2/09

EYE ON
Art

ART CONSERVATION

by Hal Marcovitz

LUCENT BOOKS
An imprint of Thomson Gale, a part of The Thomson Corporation

THOMSON
GALE™

Detroit • New York • San Francisco • San Diego • New Haven, Conn.
Waterville, Maine • London • Munich

© 2007 Thomson Gale, a part of The Thomson Corporation.

Thomson and Star Logo are trademarks and Gale and Lucent Books are registered trademarks used herein under license.

For more information, contact
Lucent Books
27500 Drake Rd.
Farmington Hills, MI 48331-3535
Or you can visit our Internet site at http://www.gale.com

LIBRARY OF CONGRESS CATALOGING-IN-PUBLICATION DATA

Marcovitz, Hal.
  Art conservation / by Hal Marcovitz.
      p. cm. — (Eye on art)
  Includes bibliographical references and index.
  ISBN 1-59018-964-7 (hard cover : alk. paper) 1. Art—Conservation and restoration—Juvenile literature. I. Title. II. Series.
  N8560.M334 2006
  702.8'8—dc22
                                                                    2006007931

Printed in the United States of America

CONTENTS

Foreword

"Art has no other purpose than to brush aside . . . everything that veils reality from us in order to bring us face to face with reality itself."

—French philosopher Henri-Louis Bergson

Some thirty-one thousand years ago, early humans painted strikingly sophisticated images of horses, bison, rhinoceroses, bears, and other animals on the walls of a cave in southern France. The meaning of these elaborate pictures is unknown, although some experts speculate that they held ceremonial significance. Regardless of their intended purpose, the Chauvet-Pont-d'Arc cave paintings represent some of the first known expressions of the artistic impulse.

From the Paleolithic era to the present day, human beings have continued to create works of visual art. Artists have developed painting, drawing, sculpture, engraving, and many other techniques to produce visual representations of landscapes, the human form, religious and historical events, and countless other subjects. The artistic impulse also finds expression in glass, jewelry, and new forms inspired by new technology. Indeed, judging by humanity's prolific artistic output throughout history, one must conclude that the compulsion to produce art is an inherent aspect of being human, and the results are among humanity's greatest cultural achievements: masterpieces such as the architectural marvels of ancient Greece, Michelangelo's perfectly rendered statue *David*, Vincent van Gogh's visionary painting *Starry Night*, and endless other treasures.

The creative impulse serves many purposes for society. At its most basic level, art is a form of entertainment or the means for a satisfying or pleasant aesthetic experience. But art's true power lies not in its potential to entertain and delight but in its ability to enlighten, to reveal the truth, and by doing so to uplift the human spirit and transform the human race.

One of the primary functions of art has been to serve religion. For most of Western history, for example, artists were paid by the church to produce works with religious themes and subjects. Art was thus a tool to help human beings transcend mundane, secular reality and achieve spiritual enlightenment. One of the best-known, and largest-scale, examples of Christian religious art is the Sistine Chapel in the Vatican in Rome. In 1508 Pope Julius II commissioned Italian Renaissance artist Michelangelo to paint the chapel's vaulted ceiling, an area of 640 square yards (535 sq. m). Michelangelo spent four years on scaffolding, his neck craned, creating a panoramic fresco of some three hundred human figures. His paintings depict Old Testament prophets and heroes, sibyls of Greek mythology, and nine scenes from the Book of Genesis, including the Creation of Adam, the Fall of Adam and Eve from the Garden of Eden, and the Flood. The ceiling of the Sistine Chapel is considered one of the greatest works of Western art and has inspired the awe of countless Christian pilgrims and other religious seekers. As eighteenth-century German poet and author Johann Wolfgang von Goethe wrote, "Until you have seen this Sistine Chapel, you can have no adequate conception of what man is capable of."

In addition to inspiring religious fervor, art can serve as a force for social change. Artists are among the visionaries of any culture. As such, they often perceive injustice and wrongdoing and confront others by reflecting what they see in their work. One classic example of art as social commentary was created in May 1937, during the brutal Spanish civil war. On May 1 Spanish artist Pablo Picasso learned of the recent attack on the small Basque village of Guernica by German airplanes allied with fascist forces led by Francisco Franco. The German pilots had used the village for target practice, a three-hour bombing that killed sixteen hundred civilians. Picasso, living in Paris, channeled his outrage over the massacre into his painting *Guernica,* a black, white, and gray mural that depicts dismembered animals and fractured human figures whose faces are contorted in agonized expressions. Initially, critics and the public condemned the painting as an incoherent hodgepodge, but the work soon came to be seen as a powerful antiwar statement and remains an iconic symbol of the violence and terror that dominated world events during the remainder of the twentieth century.

The impulse to create art—whether painting animals with crude pigments on a cave wall, sculpting a human form from marble, or commemorating human tragedy in a mural—thus serves many purposes. It offers an entertaining diversion, nourishes the imagination and the spirit, decorates and beautifies the world, and chronicles the age. But underlying all these functions is the desire to reveal that which is obscure—to illuminate, clarify, and perhaps ennoble. As Picasso himself stated, "The purpose of art is washing the dust of daily life off our souls."

The Eye on Art series is intended to assist readers in understanding the various roles of art in society. Each volume offers an in-depth exploration of a major artistic movement, medium, figure, or profession. All books in the series are beautifully illustrated with full-color photographs and diagrams. Riveting narrative, clear technical explanation, informative sidebars, fully documented quotes, a bibliography, and a thorough index all provide excellent starting points for research and discussion. With these features, the Eye on Art series is a useful introduction to the world of art—a world that can offer both insight and inspiration.

Introduction

Why Preserve Art?

Art has always been one of the pillars of civilization. Today, works of art that survive from ancient times often provide historians with a clear picture of the past. The ancient Greeks understood the lasting influence of art; the writer and physician Hippocrates once said, "Life is short, the art long."[1]

Even though the institution of art has endured over the years, many paintings, sculptures, and other works have suffered damage. Centuries of wear can harm delicate works of art. Paint peels and flakes. Marble, granite, bronze, and other hard materials used in sculpture often crack or erode over time, especially if the sculpture is displayed outdoors. Photographs fade, tapestries fray, and ceramics chip. Sometimes, art is damaged by vandalism or terrorism or simply by a clumsy mover. It is the duty—and the art—of the conservator to take damaged works of art and make them whole again.

The conservator has three distinct duties: to examine the object and document its significance, to take whatever steps are required to arrest its deterioration, and to restore the piece to its original condition with as little impact on the creator's work as possible. Unlike most other artists, the conservator strives not to be noticed. The conservator's role is to repair the damage and make it look as though nothing was wrong in the first place. The conservator labors in anonymity, desiring to leave no personal mark on a painting or other work of art.

Secrets of Ancient Civilizations

It is important to preserve art because art serves as one of the few links between modern times and the secrets of ancient civilizations. Most other forms of communication that provide an insight into the past are relatively new. The printing press was not invented until 1440, meaning that no published book, newspaper, or journal is more than a few hundred years old. Photography was born in the 1830s. Cinema is just a little more than a century old. Television did not arrive until the twentieth century. Computers did not start recording data until the 1930s.

Art, on the other hand, has been around for thousands of years and this means that the stories told by the artists have endured through history. In fact, archaeologists have found drawings on cave walls that are believed to date from the Paleolithic period, some thirty thousand years ago. Archaeologists have learned a lot from cave art, such as how early

Art conservators clean a fragile seventeenth-century Italian tapestry called "The Crucifixion" at a New York City textile conservation lab.

People have been creating art for thousands of years as can be seen in this cave painting from Algeria. The scene is thought to have been painted between 4000 B.C. and 2000 B.C.

humans hunted, farmed, and waged war. Says Australian archaeologist Robert G. Bednarik, "Prehistoric rock art is by far the largest body of evidence we have of humanity's artistic, cognitive and cultural beginnings. . . . This massive, semi-permanent and cumulative record is the most direct evidence we have of how pre-humans first became human and then evolved complex social systems."[2]

High-Tech Resources and Skills

Archaeologists are continually surprised at how well rock art on cave walls has held up after thousands of years. Many images of horses, bison, deer, mammoths, and other animals are surprisingly clear and still colorful. Unfortunately, paintings, sculptures, and other pieces of art fashioned in the centuries since those primitive drawings are often in some state of decay. Indeed, every work of art begins to deteriorate the moment it is completed. The damage may take centuries or occur quite rapidly. Some collectors of modern art are alarmed to find colors fading and other signs of deterioration after owning their pieces for just a few years. Many artists who are still working are gracious enough to repair the damage to their own paintings—a dab of paint here or there often fixes the problem. Former art critic Daniel Grant recalls one artist, Norwegian portraitist Odd Nerdrum, who was so dismayed when told that the colors in one of his paintings had faded that he rehired the model and painted the portrait again, then presented the new piece to the collector. "Nerdrum isn't the only artist who tries to make amends for work that doesn't hold up, although few will go to such lengths,"[3] says Grant.

In all other cases, museums, galleries, and private owners turn to conservators to repair damaged artwork. They use a variety of methods, often calling on high-tech resources and carefully developed skills to re-create what the artist originally rendered. Certainly, modern conservators need to know a lot about art and art history, but they also need to know a lot about computer-assisted imaging, laser technology, infrared photography, chemical analysis, and other scientific fields. Indeed, art conservation is a dynamic profession, continually changing as new methods of preservation and rehabilitation are developed.

And as the work of the conservator improves, so does the likelihood that a work of art will endure for hundreds of years or more, giving many generations of people the opportunity to observe, study, and enjoy the work of the artist. The conservator may thus become as important to the life of a piece of art as the artist who produced it. Says Columbia University art history professor James Beck, "Those men and women engaged in the study, conservation and maintenance of the art and cultural objects of the past . . . perform a laudable activity that warrants the admiration and support of society. Their roles should be understood as vital components in the preservation of the integrity of the artists, named or anonymous, whose works they are seeking to preserve."[4]

The Art and the Science of Conservation

For centuries, craftsmen who repaired art relied on home-grown techniques they acquired as apprentices or through trial and error on their own. Art "restorers" were usually artists themselves and had little understanding of the chemical composition of pigments and other materials. They had no reason to explore such wider issues as why those substances deteriorated over time. They performed their restorations using processes and materials that were unlikely to last more than a few years.

It has only been during the past century that art conservators have distinguished themselves from art restorers. Certainly, art conservation requires great artistic skill, but art conservators must also have a strong background in the sciences, because science has become vitally important in the conservation of art.

In America, the scientific approach to art conservation did not start until the 1920s, when museums first started adding chemists and other scientists to their staffs. Since then, the science of art conservation has become well established. Many large museums now employ staffs of scientifically oriented conservators and provide them with sophisticated equipment. Despite the emphasis on science, there is no question that the

While working on a Spanish cathedral, art restorers discovered this Renaissance angel fresco, which had been covered up for over three hundred years.

profession remains very much an art that requires a steady hand, an eye for color, and an artist's vision. Says Smithsonian Institution conservator Konstanze Bachmann,

> Conservation today is a scientifically informed discipline guided by general principles as well as by a growing body of written information. This is not to suggest that conservation is a science. Scientific investigation and research have greatly contributed to a better understanding of the process of deterioration and have provided safer methods of testing and treatment; however, only the sensitivity, knowledge, integrity, and skill of an individual can make possible a synthesis of science and art.[5]

Early Techniques

Contemporary art conservators are constantly coming across paintings, sculptures, and other works of art in which well-meaning restorers working decades or even centuries ago employed techniques that failed to stand the test of time. Using the techniques and materials available to them, the old restorers tried various homegrown methods in their effort to clean the grime that accumulated on the surface of art. During the 1700s, one common method was to use table wine as a cleaner. Initially, the coating of wine did make the painting sparkle, but the wine also left a film on the surface that became evident over a period of years.

Not only were the restorers scrubbing art with table wine but unless they worked outdoors it is likely they labored over the canvases by candlelight. Years ago, candles were made of tallow, or rendered animal fat. As the tallow burned, the smoke wafted through the room, leaving a greasy layer on the surface of the art.

Finally, after cleaning the paintings, the restorers applied a varnish, or sealant, to the surfaces. Typically, the varnishes were concocted from fat-based greases, glues, and oils. Invariably, the layer of sealant darkened over the years or became brittle and cracked, causing damage to the paint surface below.

Sometimes, the craftsmen were just not very good at their craft. If they failed to clean a painting properly before varnishing, they trapped dirt beneath the layer of varnish. They often used materials that were simply unsuitable for the task at hand. Medieval art expert and author Daniel V. Thompson cites a typical case in which the restorer applied a varnish commonly used for the wood and chrome components of coaches to the wall art, or frescoes, at an ancient monastery:

> Some fifty of sixty years ago, a very high-minded but misguided Englishman who admired greatly the seventh-century paintings on the walls of the cave temples at Ajanta, the matchless Buddhist monastery in Hyderabad

Attempts to preserve the cave paintings at Ajanta in India with varnish proved disastrous and irreversible.

State in Central India, undertook to protect and improve some of his favorites there by applying to them a coat of really good coach varnish. It was the best varnish. But those paintings . . . were as nearly as possible pure pigment, almost as fresh and delicate as pastel, and putting varnish on them most unhappily made oil paintings of them. . . . The varnish, in that half-lit cave, turned very dark indeed, and those responsible for the upkeep of the caves determined to try to remove it. An expert in the treatment of frescoes was called in from Italy. I saw the work . . . and realized how hopeless it was to hope for restitution. The damage could not be undone.[6]

Still, given what was known about paints and other artists' materials, the restoration was usually welcomed by the client. After all, the cleaning, retouching, and revarnishing usually did initially improve the painting. Only after years or decades of

The Giza pyramids in Egypt were royal tombs for the pharaohs. Inset, an ancient sculpture of the goddess Isis protects King Tutankhamen.

hanging in a museum, gallery, or private home did the restorer's work start deteriorating. By then, it is likely the original owner had either died or sold the painting and the new owner had no idea how radiant the original may have appeared.

Science and Conservation

Starting in the nineteenth century, museums started to pay a lot of attention to the deterioration of their exhibits, although their first efforts at conservation did not address damage to art. This was the era in which archaeologists traipsed through the jungles of Africa, the deserts of the Middle East, and the mysterious corners of the Orient, uncovering all manner of ancient relics. Masks worn by African tribesmen, pottery used by Mesopotamians, sarcophagi holding the mummies of Egyptian princes, jade idols carved by ancient Chinese artisans, and other examples of what are known as ethnographic relics were unearthed and sent to museums in Europe, where curators hoped to put them on exhibit. To make them worthy of display and to help historians understand the significance of the finds, conservators were called in to clean the relics and analyze the materials used to produce them.

Meanwhile, in the United States, Harvard University recognized the importance of science in art conservation by establishing a Department of Conservation and Technical Research at the university's Fogg Art Museum. It was the first art museum in America to create a separate conservation department. Since it was affiliated with Harvard, the department's conservators could call on the university's vast resources in both the sciences and the arts to help them solve many artistic mysteries. When the department was established in 1929, the Fogg's director, Edward W. Forbes, hired a chemist and an X-ray specialist for the staff. An X-ray image of a painting enabled conservators to see beneath the layers of paint, allowing them to discover a great deal about the composition and deterioration of the work. The Fogg also published a journal, *Technical Studies in the Field of Fine Arts*, which became the first scholarly journal for art conservators. It meant that conservators

EDWARD W. FORBES

The individual most responsible for introducing scientific techniques to art conservation in America was Edward W. Forbes, director of Harvard University's Fogg Art Museum from 1909 to 1944. Forbes was born in Boston, Massachusetts, to a privileged family. His father was the business partner of Alexander Graham Bell. His mother was the daughter of poet Ralph Waldo Emerson. Educated at Harvard, Forbes discovered a love for art while traveling in Europe. Upon returning home, he joined a committee of the Fogg charged with persuading Harvard's wealthy alumni to donate or lend their paintings to the museum.

After his appointment as director, Forbes guided the expansion of the Fogg that included construction of a new home for the museum in 1927 and development of the first American art conservation laboratory in 1929. Forbes was fascinated with art history and believed that science could expand the understanding of art and its origins.

He was also an early opponent of censorship. In 1911, the Fogg hosted an exhibit of the work of painter Edgar Degas, which included some nudes. Despite opposition from members of proper Boston society, Forbes insisted on scheduling the Degas exhibit. To one critic, he wrote, "I think this show is an excellent thing for the Fogg Museum. It is bringing hundreds of people into the building who would never come before and who, perhaps, could have been reached in no other way except by a modern show."

Patrons walk through the Fogg Art Museum, the first art museum to create a conservation department.

Quoted in *Harvard Magazine*, "Mad for Degas," July–August 2005. www.harvardmagazine.com/on-line/070592.html.

could now publish information about their projects and techniques, sharing developments in the advancement of their craft with other conservators.

The Gettysburg Cyclorama

The Fogg Art Museum also served as the nation's first training academy for art conservators, who eventually left the Fogg's staff for positions at other museums and cultural institutions. Several former Fogg conservators found jobs with the National Park Service. In addition to its responsibility for managing the nation's parks and historic sites, the Park Service is entrusted with the care of thousands of objects of art owned by the federal government. Many of those pieces are displayed in the White House, the U.S. Capitol, and other federal buildings.

One of the Park Service's most significant projects was the 1959 restoration of the gargantuan Gettysburg cyclorama, a painting 27 feet (8m) high and 353 feet (108m) wide depicting the failed infantry assault led by Confederate general George E. Pickett during the Battle of Gettysburg. The cyclorama was designed to be viewed from the center of a circular room, surrounding the visitor in a 360-degree panorama. The cyclorama, which is named *The Battle of Gettysburg*, was painted in 1884 by French artist Paul Dominique Philippoteaux. It weighs 3 tons (2.7m tons).

The cyclorama was regarded as an amazing artistic achievement. Indeed, people had never seen a piece of art so large. Certainly, they had never seen a painting that attempted to tell such a vivid story—the failure of Pickett's charge turned the tide in the battle, resulting in a sweeping Union victory. When the cyclorama was unveiled, people waited in line fourteen hours a day, seven days a week, to see Philippoteaux's dramatic retelling of the battle. Wrote a journalist who saw the painting,

> The effect . . . is simply astounding. [The viewer] finds himself upon a high hill, with a stretch of forty miles of country all around him and everywhere within range of his vision, on the hills, in the valleys, in the woods, on the open fields, in ditches and behind stone walls, and

Standing before a detail of the 360-degree Gettysburg cyclorama, an art conservator discusses the restoration of the 1884 painting.

in shot-shattered shanties he beholds the soldiers of the blue and gray engaged in the awful struggle for the supremacy. . . . It must be seen to be fully appreciated.[7]

The painting was exhibited in Boston for some twenty years, then obtained by a New Jersey department store owner who displayed it in his store for two years. The owner then erected a specially designed building on Baltimore Street in Gettysburg, Pennsylvania, to exhibit the work. By the time the cyclorama went on display in Gettysburg in 1913, it was already in need of attention. Philippoteaux had painted the picture on strips of canvas that were pieced together to form the finished work. Several of the canvas panels were ripped while other panels sustained rot from contact with moisture. Conservators repaired the rips and replaced the rotted portions with new pieces of canvas, which were then repainted by artists to match Philippoteaux's work. Still, the cyclorama suffered additional damage as it endured years of display in a public building.

Forty-three years after its last restoration, Paul Philippoteaux's *The Battle of Gettysburg* is once again in need of repair. In late 2005, art conservators commenced a $9 million project to restore the huge painting.

The cyclorama is suffering from some of the same ills that afflicted it during its last restoration, from 1959 to 1962. Conservators have found tears in the canvas as well as many places where the paint is flaking off the surface. Also, 15 feet (4.5m) of blue sky that were lost before the last restoration will be repainted by muralists.

When the cyclorama is rehung it will have a new home—a modern museum and visitors' center that is part of a $95 million project at Gettysburg National Military Park in Pennsylvania. Again, a special round room has been designed to display the cyclorama in a 360-degree panorama. The new home for the cyclorama is slated to open in 2007.

In the former visitors' center, visitors viewed the painting from below because the cyclorama was displayed above floor level. The new facility will have a raised floor so that visitors may view the cyclorama on a plane even with the action of the battle depicted in the picture. Says Robert C. Wilburn, president of the Gettysburg National Battlefield Museum Foundation, "We're trying to get as close as we can to creating the illusion of being in the cyclorama in 1884. You'll get that total-immersion experience."

Visitors stand back to absorb the enormous Gettysburg cyclorama.

Quoted in Lisanne Renner, "For the Painted Soldiers of Gettysburg, the War Is Now Against Time," *New York Times*, November 16, 2005.

The National Park Service acquired the cyclorama as well as its building in the 1940s. The cyclorama was kept on display in the old Baltimore Street facility until it was taken down in 1959 in preparation for hanging in a new visitors' center that would be opened at Gettysburg National Military Park three years later. The visitors' center included a circular building designed to display the cyclorama. When Philippoteaux's work was taken off the walls of the Baltimore Street building, it was evident that the painting was in need of a major conservation effort.

To begin the restoration, the conservation crew lined the entire face of the painting with sheets of tissue paper to hold loose paint in place while the artwork was moved. Next, conservators recut the cyclorama into strips 20 feet (6m) wide so that each panel would fit on a specially built padded work table. The strips were placed face down so that wrinkles in the canvas could be smoothed out through the application of heat and moisture.

The conservators then went to work on the canvas, repairing tears and mending old repairs. Once the repair work was completed, they glued a layer of fresh canvas to the back of the old canvas in a process known as relining. Since the new canvas had to be stretched before the wax-based glue could be applied, it required the development of a special apparatus designed to stretch the large sheets of fabric. Once the canvas was relined, the strips were turned over, enabling the conservators to clean a painted surface of some 10,000 square feet (930 sq. m) that had accumulated decades' worth of grime. Each inch was scrubbed by hand using gauze pads dipped in cleaning solutions. Three years after it was stripped off the walls of the old Baltimore Street building, *The Battle of Gettysburg* was rehung in the park's new visitors' center.

High-Tech Tools

Restoration of *The Battle of Gettysburg* showed just how far American conservators had advanced their art and science in the thirty-three years since Harvard's Fogg Art Museum established the first full-time staff of conservators. Certainly,

Conservators in Italy work at a vacuum table during restoration of a bronze sculpture.

the development of the craft did not end there. By the 1970s, most museum conservation departments were investing in expensive equipment that had been designed specifically for the work of art conservators. The development of the vacuum table was an important advancement—paintings, photographs, and other works could be held flat and stationary by suction while the conservator worked. Now, there was no need to tape down a piece of art and risk damage to the original when the tape was removed. In recent years, improvements to the vacuum table have included the addition of translucent domes that can be lowered over the whole table to control temperature and humidity. To work on the piece, the conservator wears gloves attached to the inside of the dome—much the same way as a worker in a nuclear plant handles radioactive material behind a protective shield.

A visitor entering a well-equipped art conservation laboratory would also find an array of microscopes that help conservators perform many functions. For example, at the Fogg Art

Museum's conservation department, which is now known as the Straus Center for Conservation, staff members use microscopes to inspect the tiniest details of paintings and other works. Fogg conservators have used microscopes to inspect metal sculptures, searching for similarities in how the sculptures were cast. When the origin of a sculpture is unknown, finding even the tiniest similarities in casting techniques can help conservators identify the artists.

Microscopes can also be used to identify the origin of paintings. Each artist has a unique way of using a brush, just as each person has a unique way of signing his or her name. To help identify the artist, a microscope can detect the intricacies of each brush stroke. Also, microscopes can disclose deterioration in a painting—such as tiny cracks—that is not visible to the unaided eye.

A well-equipped conservation lab will employ a scanning electron microscope, which bombards the surface of a painting with electrons. The electrons may be absorbed by the painting

A scanning electron microscope can help conservators reveal brush strokes, deterioration, and even the chemical makeup of the materials used to create the work.

or reflected, or they may cause the painting to emit other electrons. The microscope then records all that activity in an image of the painting, providing information to the conservators on the chemical makeup of the materials used to create the artwork. That can be an enormously effective tool for a conservator who must decide what types of chemicals are best to clean the painting's surface.

Seeing Things More Clearly

Sometimes, the scanning electron microscope can yield a surprise. At the National Gallery of Art in Washington, conservators using an electron microscope studied the 1617 oil painting *St. Cecilia and an Angel* by Orazio Gentileschi. The electron microscope revealed that part of the image contained a lead-based yellow paint while the yellow paint in a different part was composed of lead, tin, and the metal hardener known as antimony. That piece of information led curators at the National Gallery to determine that a second artist, whom they identified as Giovanni Lanfranco, painted over some of Gentileschi's original image. Therefore, the painting is now attributed to both artists.

Conservators still use X-rays to look below layers of paint, but now have additional methods that help them see things even more clearly. At the Straus Center conservators employ infrared reflectography to look beneath paint and grime. Different layers of paint absorb infrared light differently, depending on the composition of the paints. A camera that records infrared light can look through a painting layer by layer, all the way down to the artist's sketches on the canvas.

A recent infrared examination of the 1508 Leonardo da Vinci painting *The Madonna of the Rocks* at the National Gallery in London revealed sketches the artist made for a far different painting than the one he ultimately completed. The painting depicts the Virgin Mary in a dark cave, cradling the baby Jesus and surrounded by angels. The drawings beneath the surface show a kneeling woman, one hand folded across her chest, the other extended. Says National Gallery researcher

The use of infrared reflectography allowed conservators to see drawings beneath the surface of *The Madonna of the Rocks* by Leonardo da Vinci.

Rachel Billinge, "It was an extraordinary moment when we shone the camera on the Madonna's face—just to get the settings right because the paint was thin there—and instantly we saw a hand which had no place there. We all had to go away and sit quietly for a bit, just to get our thoughts in order."[8]

Once the job of assessing how the art was produced and what has gone wrong with the piece is completed, conservators can employ modern methods to clean and restore the work. Years ago, conservators removed old paint flakes by using a pair of tweezers, which might pull off more paint than the conservator intended. Now, lasers are used to burn off old paint, so conservators never have to touch the fragile paint with their hands or mechanical instruments.

Spectroscopy and Spit-Cleaning

Advances in chemistry have also helped conservators clean and repair art. Development of new chemicals for art conservation has helped make paints and other materials last longer and sealants stay transparent and glossy longer.

At the National Gallery of Art, conservators used a chemical process to restore a fourteenth-century ciborium, a glass and copper container used by Catholic priests during communion services. To analyze the composition of the materials used in the ciborium, conservators employed a process known as X-ray fluorescence spectroscopy, which involves measuring the wavelengths of X-rays as they are bounced off different metals. Since the different metals produce different wave-

Using X-Ray Light to Uncover a Painting's Layers

A. X-Ray light is applied evenly to the surface of a painting.
B. Light exposes the images as well as the paint layers beneath it.
C. A camera can take a photograph of the various paint layers.

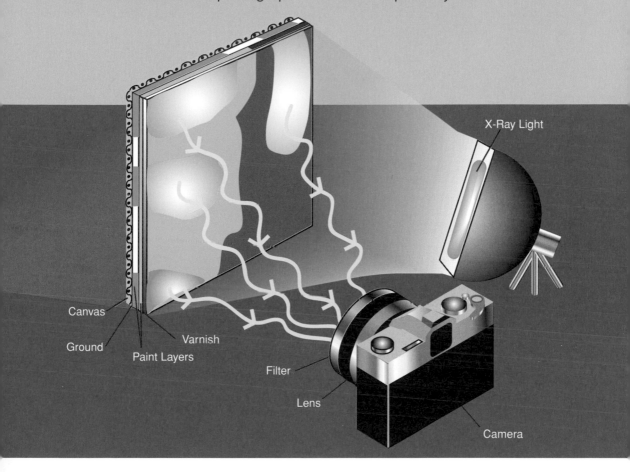

X-Ray Light

Canvas

Ground

Varnish

Paint Layers

Filter

Lens

Camera

lengths, the conservators could tell the chemical content of the ciborium by the wavelengths it produced. The process told the conservators that one piece of glass in the ciborium had a high lead content while another piece had a high potassium content. Since potassium is very unstable and becomes brittle in dry climates, the conservators recommended that the ciborium be displayed in a sealed case in which a humid climate could be maintained.

Conservators today also use some rather low-tech chemical processes that were known many years ago. In 2005, conservators restored a mural called *Before the White Man Came* that had deteriorated during the seventy-two years it hung in the Saskatchewan Legislative Building in Canada. To clean off the grime, conservators used cotton swabs moistened with their own saliva. Conservator Tara Fraser said, "We're going to spit-clean the entire painting. The enzymes that help to break down food before it goes into the digestive system are found in saliva and are actually really good cleaning agents."[9]

"One-to-One"

As the conservators working on the Saskatchewan mural have shown, some old techniques still have their place in art conservation, although fat-based varnishes have been discarded and nobody cleans art with table wine anymore. Many of the old techniques have been replaced by vacuum tables, electron

Art conservators carefully restore a ceiling painting in the Catherine Palace in Russia. The painstaking work has taken a decade to complete.

microscopes, lasers, X-ray fluorescence spectroscopy, and infrared reflectography. Art conservation, however, is still very much an art. Those sophisticated devices may provide insight into the project and guide the conservator's hand, but the conservator must still treat each damaged work of art as a unique problem to be solved. Says Andrew Oddy, keeper of conservation at the British Museum in London, "Science has thus made a tremendous contribution to the materials and methods of conservation . . . but hardly any processes have yet been discovered which are adaptable to mass-treatment. . . . Conservation still relies almost entirely on a one-to-one relationship between the object and the conservator."[10] Thus a steady hand and an eye for color are as important today as they were in the days when paintings were cleaned by candlelight.

When Good Art Goes Bad

There are dozens of reasons why artwork suffers damage. Even the world's most important works of art can be affected. Art can be damaged by the deterioration of the materials used in its creation. Paintings, sculptures, and other works of art can suffer from forces of nature, such as changes in temperature and moisture in the air. Artworks can also be harmed by infestation by mice or insects, wayward brooms or vacuum cleaners, and even the clumsy efforts of owners to clean their own paintings.

Before conservators begin the process of repairing the damage, they must understand why the deterioration occurred. In some works of art—such as Michelangelo's frescoes on the ceiling of the Vatican's Sistine Chapel—damage occurs over a period of centuries and can be attributed to factors ranging from mistakes made by the artist to a leaky roof. In fact, the damage in the Sistine Chapel frescoes started showing up even before Michelangelo completed them in 1512. To preserve the ceiling, the Vatican created the position of *mundator*, which means "cleaner." According to Andrew Oddy of the British Museum, the mundator's charge was to keep the frescoes free "from the dust and other filth, and also from the smoke of the

Before restoration, the Sistine Chapel frescoes were covered with centuries of dirt and grime but now the colors are glowing and vibrant.

lamps."[11] The task was well beyond the powers of the mundator: A recent long-term project to clean Michelangelo's masterpiece found the ceiling of the Sistine Chapel caked in grime.

Deterioration of the Sistine Chapel

At the epicenter of the Vatican in Rome stands St. Peter's Basilica, built in the 1470s. In 1508, Pope Julius II directed the era's most eminent artist, Michelangelo, to cover the ceiling of the basilica's Sistine Chapel with images from the Bible, most notably the stories of the Creation, Adam and Eve, and the Flood. Michelangelo spent four years—as the story goes, lying on his back atop scaffolding—painting the frescoes that are today among the most important and familiar works of art in the world. After some five centuries of neglect, it took conservators working in the 1980s and 1990s more than a decade to clean and repair them.

Things started going wrong even as Michelangelo worked. The artist used too much water in some of the pigments. As Michelangelo painted scenes from the Flood, mildew started forming on the plaster ceiling. Michelangelo, who had reluctantly accepted the commission to paint the frescoes—he regarded himself as a sculptor, not a painter—hoped the evidence of mildew would convince Julius of the futility of the project. "Indeed, I told Your Holiness that this is not my art; what I have done is spoiled,"[12] fumed the artist. Julius was adamant, though, and ordered Michelangelo to continue.

Michelangelo completed the ceiling in 1512. Within a few years, damage started showing up in the image of the Prophet Jeremiah. The fault was not Michelangelo's. Decades after its construction, the basilica shifted on its foundation, throwing the building out of plumb—meaning its walls were now leaning slightly and its ceilings sagged. Most buildings eventually slip out of plumb as the construction materials expand and contract due to moisture in the air and ground. In most buildings, the difference is virtually invisible—perhaps a door sticks or a win-

dow does not open or close properly. In St. Peter's Basilica, the slight shift proved disastrous. When the ceiling of the basilica sagged, some of the plaster cracked. In the Sistine Chapel, part of the image of Jeremiah broke off and fell to the floor below.

St. Peter's Basilica, which houses many art treasures including the ceiling of the Sistine Chapel, is shown in this aerial view of the Vatican.

Salt, Grime, and Tallow Grease

Typical of most artists of the era, Michelangelo mixed his own paints from metals and other minerals dug from the earth and ground into powders. He used iron oxide to make brown, cobalt and ground glass to make blue, lead oxide as his ingredient for orange, the mineral cinnabar to make red, and so on. Egg yolks were stirred into the mix to help the colors bind to the ceiling, while linseed oil was used to enhance drying. For the most part, the paints themselves worked well. They were absorbed into the ceiling and bonded chemically with the calcium and carbon in the plaster.

The problems really started when dirt and grime accumulated on the ceiling. In the years before paved roads, horses and

Computer technology aids in the restoration of the Sistine Chapel. Layers of salt residue, grime, and animal glue gradually caused the frescoes to deteriorate.

wagons stirred up lots of dust in Rome. The dust found its way into buildings, including St. Peter's Basilica.

Dust from the streets was not the only problem. Rain also damaged the ceiling of the chapel. Rome is located near the Mediterranean Sea. Rainfall in that part of Italy is heavily laden with salt. Centuries of salty rain falling on the Vatican took their toll. As the water was absorbed into the basilica and the other buildings, it left a salty residue on the walls and ceilings, causing stains. At one point, there was also a leak in the roof of the basilica. Although the leak caused no direct damage to the ceiling of the Sistine Chapel, it did provide a direct path for the salt to enter the building.

The Sistine conservators also found a layer of glue composed of animal fat slathered across the ceiling. The glue was applied as a sealant and also to brighten the images, giving them a glossy finish. At first, the idea worked, but over time the glue hardened and shrank, and tiny pieces started falling to the floor. As the glue fell it pulled chunks of plaster out of the ceiling, damaging the frescoes. Also, the gloss effect created by the glue did not last long—within a few years, the layer of glue had darkened, leaving a dull finish on top of Michelangelo's images.

To clean the ceiling, conservators first sponge-washed the surface with distilled water, which is boiled to remove impurities. Next, a chemical cleaning solution was applied with a natural fiber brush. Two of the ingredients in the cleaning solution were bicarbonates of sodium and ammonium, which are often used as household cleaners. The bicarbonates and other ingredients were applied in gel form, then left on the ceiling for a few minutes so they could absorb the grime. The gel was then sponged off the ceiling, leaving a clean surface.

Sometimes, when the grime was lifted off, the conservators uncovered holes in the plaster. These were patched and contemporary paints employed to touch up the frescoes. In addition, environmental controls were installed in the basilica to regulate the temperature and humidity and filter the air.

Painting on Canvas and Wood

Michelangelo's frescoes suffered from the type of deterioration unique to paintings that are rendered onto plaster ceilings. Much more common forms of painted art were also vulnerable to decay. Centuries ago, most artists painted on stretched canvases, as artists do today, or on panels of wood that were glued together, then slathered with a priming layer of chalk mixed with glue made from animal fat. The paint was then applied to that surface, which was known as the ground layer. Ground layers were also applied to canvases. Over time, deterioration of the canvases and wood panels caused damage to the art.

The wood panels, for example, were joined edge to edge, then glued. Over the years, the wood might warp or the glue would dry out and crack, causing the panels to separate. Usually, changes in atmospheric conditions cause the warping and cracking—a humid day followed by a dry day forces the wood and the binding materials to expand and contract. Also, the ground layer often darkens, which in turn darkens the colors applied on top. That is caused by a chemical breakdown in the ingredients of the ground layer, which typically included a mixture of chalk and fat-based glues or oils. Over time, as the ground layers darkened they caused a darkening of the home-made browns, blues, oranges, and other colors applied on the surface of the painting.

Canvas is also affected by atmospheric conditions. The fabric used for canvas was usually linen, cotton, or hemp. Like wood, canvas expands and contracts due to moisture in the air. Those slight changes can cause the canvas to sag or tighten and even tear. Also, canvas was often glued to wood panels. The glue would bleed through the canvas, causing the paint on the other side to flake off. Centuries ago, art restorers who saw this damage occurring took steps to reline the canvas—they reinforced the old canvas by taking it off the wood panel and attaching a second layer of canvas beneath the original. Like many techniques practiced by restorers in the past, relining provided a short-term solution but, in the long term, proved disastrous. According to David Bomford, a senior restorer at London's National Gallery of Art,

> The traditional method of attaching a lining was to use animal glues and hot tailors' irons. Expertly done, this alarming technique could achieve satisfactory results. However, the old methods could also do much harm by scorching, crushing and scraping the paint layers. A good deal of the damage to paintings uncovered by today's restorers and blamed on over-cleaning was, in fact, caused by past liners and subsequently concealed by repaint.[13]

Laborious Effort

Today, conservators fix flaking or cracked paint by applying glue in a laborious process known as facing. A very thin sheet of paper known as Japan paper is placed over a small section of the painting; then glue is painted over the Japan paper. Because the paper is so thin glue seeps through in an even layer. Finally,

WARPS IN THE *MONA LISA*

ven the most scrupulous care does not save old works of art from deterioration. Leonardo da Vinci's *Mona Lisa*—perhaps the most famous painting in the world—is kept in a climate-controlled glass display case in the Paris art museum known as the Louvre, where some 6 million visitors a year stop to inspect the five hundred-year-old painting.

Once a year, the *Mona Lisa* is taken out of the case for an inspection. In 2004, the inspection revealed that the painting's wood panels are warping. The warp was detected in the center of the painting and may have been caused by two wood braces added to the back of the painting in the seventeenth century to prevent expansion of a small crack. The braces are made of a different wood than the painting's panels. The two woods react to age differently, thus causing the warp.

Louvre officials are concerned. If the warping continues, it could damage the paint surface. They hope to reverse the warping by manipulating the back of the panels. Conservators have already decided that they will not retouch the *Mona Lisa*. They believe that no other artist should take a paintbrush to da Vinci's masterpiece.

Louvre museum employees take down the Mona Lisa *painting for its annual inspection. The 2004 review found warps in the wood panels.*

a weight is placed atop the Japan paper while the glue dries. When the glue has dried, the weight is removed and the Japan paper is peeled off the painting. The excess glue is then peeled off the painting.

Sometimes, the paint flakes because of "pockets" that have formed under the painted surface—these are particularly common in paintings done on wood panels. As the name suggests, pockets are tiny bubbles that have formed between the paint and the wood. The paint has not yet flaked but is in danger of doing so because there is now a bubble of air between the paint and the surface. To glue down paint that has formed a pocket, the conservator heats or moistens a small area of the painting that surrounds the pocket. This makes the surface of the painting supple enough so that it will not crack when the bubble is pressed down. The glue is then applied to the surface through a layer of Japan paper. Finally, the conservator applies pressure by using a flat instrument such as a palette knife.

An art conservator uses a sheet of Japan paper to mend this badly torn page from a Byzantine writing tablet.

Sometimes, the paints caused problems. Homemade pigments were often not absorbed well by the canvas or wood panels. Over time, this caused colors to fade. It was also common for artists to paint over mistakes or, if they were not satisfied with the composition, to change the model's pose and paint over the old image. As the colors fade, the original images can show through. Fading colors can also reveal the original sketches because the charcoal marks made by the artist bleed through the paint. When conservators repair paintings with faded or washed-out colors, they may have to add new paint to the surface to touch up the images.

Also, as the paints absorb moisture in the air and then dry out, they expand and contract. Tiny cracks form

in the picture. This phenomenon, known as craquelure, can dominate the image. Craquelure can also occur if a fragile painting is bumped during transit.

Craquelure is repaired by applying a putty to fill the cracks. There is one way conservators apply putty and that is by hand. Typically, conservators use brushes, knives, tiny spatulas, or even their fingers to work the putty into the grooves on the surface of the painting, although vacuums and dryers can be used later to help the putty adhere to the surface and harden. Still, the process of filling is decidedly low-tech. For example, conservators often use damp pieces of cork to perform the function known as leveling off, which flattens the putty.

After the putty is applied, the conservator will use paint to touch up the surface. In most cases, several layers go atop the putty. Conservators know that the color of the putty is important—it must match the ground layer so that the paint applied on top of the putty has a better chance of matching the pigments used by the artist.

The artist's final step in creating a painting was to brush on a layer of varnish to seal the work and, ironically, protect it

Assisted by sophisticated equipment, conservators at the National Gallery of Art restore and maintain old paintings and other artwork.

from deterioration. As in the Sistine Chapel, the varnish was composed of animal fat, which once again proved to be no friend to the fragile pigments used to create the piece. Over time, the varnishes lost their clear gloss and instead gave the paintings a flat, dull look. In recent years, chemicals have been developed that can strip old varnish off a painting without damaging the delicate surface below. It is a process that must be performed with caution. Says David Bomford, "Removal of darkened varnishes is a delicate and painstaking process, carried out with small amounts of solvent on cotton wool swabs. Clearly, it is an operation that cannot allow the smallest margin of error."[14]

Giving Art a Suntan

Paintings and other forms of art can be damaged by what are otherwise innocent conditions, such as direct exposure to sunlight. The ultraviolet radiation in sunlight can cause the colors of a painting to fade. Andrew Oddy of the British Museum suggests that exposing art to ultraviolet light is similar to giving the human body a suntan. He says,

> Suntan and sunburn are good examples of the destructive effect of light on natural materials, but, while the skin of a living person can recover and be regenerated . . . changes produced in "dead" organic matter are irreversible. Suntan is generated most quickly in bright sunlight containing a lot of ultraviolet radiation, and similarly it is UV light which is most destructive to objects in museums. Hence museums with natural history collections, textiles, ethnographia, paintings and watercolors must control both the daylight and the UV light falling on the objects.[15]

Outdoor sculpture is highly vulnerable to sunlight as well as other natural conditions, including rain, snow, and ice. A typical example was the statue of the Greek god Eros that stood atop a fountain in downtown Liverpool, England. In 1991, the Liverpool Museum was called in to refurbish the

Stained glass is one form of art that must endure the elements. The glass is, after all, installed in windows in churches and other buildings throughout the world. The art of stained glass requires the artist to fit tiny pieces of colored glass into a pattern held together by lead strips.

There is no question that stained-glass windows are resilient; some have remained intact since medieval times. Nevertheless, when moisture, dirt, and air pollutants leak into the seals between the glass and the lead, there is usually trouble. When the deterioration of a stained-glass window is allowed to continue over a period of years, the glass can pick up a dirty film, lose its luster and grow dull, or even change colors. The glass can even become brittle and crack and fall out of the window.

Says Ernst Bacher, chair of the International Council on Monuments and Sites' Committee on Stained Glass, "Glass paintings are works of art of very high artistic value. Our efforts to preserve them will remain incomprehensible if we fail to carry out . . . restoration measures with the same care and attention as with other art forms."

Workers on scaffolding restore the stained glass windows of a chapel in Lyon, France.

Ernst Bacher, *Stained Glass.* Paris: International Council on Monuments and Sites, 1993, p. 4.

statue, which is composed of an aluminum surface fastened to a steel frame. Conservators found the aluminum skin covered with decades of grime. Also, the skin had split in many places and the steel frame was coated with rust. Inside, the statue had picked up a coating of calcium—the result of rain that seeped under the skin. Conservators used a laser to clean off the rust and calcium. In places where the statue had corroded, the old skin was cut off and replaced with new aluminum patches.

Air Pollution Causes Damage

Not only do the sun and weather cause problems for art but the air does as well—specifically, the pollution in the air. The floating chemicals and solids generated by car exhaust, factory smokestacks, and other causes of pollution can damage art, particularly if it is displayed outside. The pollutants form a caustic film on statuary, eating away the surface. Many of the world's oldest outdoor monuments, such as the Parthenon in Greece, are deteriorating because of the pollutants that coat their surfaces. Says Oddy, "Air pollution is so widespread that virtually all museum collections are at risk from it, but monuments in the open air are the most vulnerable. . . . Heritage agencies around the world are grappling with the problem."[16] Oddy believes that the only solution for the problem is to ban the use of oil, coal, and other sources of pollution.

Certainly, that is not going to happen. The conservator must therefore find ways to deal with pollution to protect outdoor art. Smithsonian Institution conservator Konstanze Bachmann points out that as pollution, acid rain, and other environmental conditions grow worse, curators may be forced to move art into a controlled environment. As the custodian of Michelangelo's frescoes, the Vatican has already taken steps to keep the Sistine Chapel in a climate-controlled and dirt-free environment. Even indoors, art can be affected by variations in temperature and humidity, as well as dust that comes in through windows and doors. In many cases it is necessary to protect art by installing air-conditioners and similar equipment to maintain a fixed and clean climate. Elsewhere, though, few museums, galleries, and private owners are likely

Causes of Damage to Museum Objects

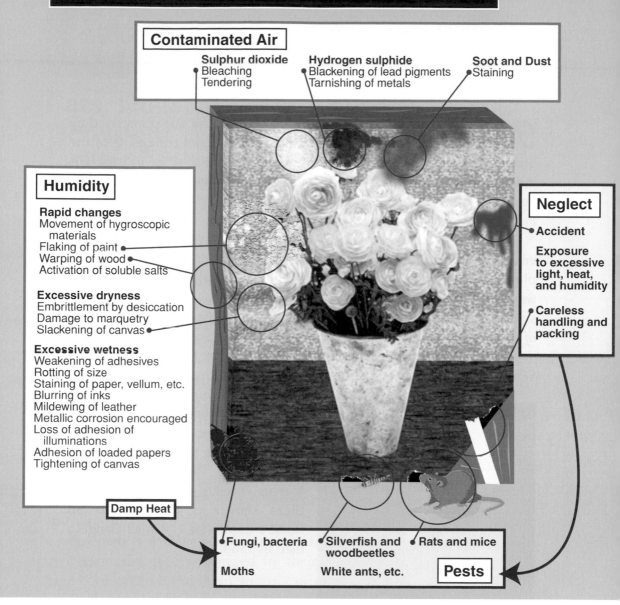

Contaminated Air

Sulphur dioxide
- Bleaching
- Tendering

Hydrogen sulphide
- Blackening of lead pigments
- Tarnishing of metals

Soot and Dust
- Staining

Humidity

Rapid changes
- Movement of hygroscopic materials
- Flaking of paint
- Warping of wood
- Activation of soluble salts

Excessive dryness
- Embrittlement by desiccation
- Damage to marquetry
- Slackening of canvas

Excessive wetness
- Weakening of adhesives
- Rotting of size
- Staining of paper, vellum, etc.
- Blurring of inks
- Mildewing of leather
- Metallic corrosion encouraged
- Loss of adhesion of illuminations
- Adhesion of loaded papers
- Tightening of canvas

Damp Heat

Neglect
- Accident

Exposure to excessive light, heat, and humidity

- Careless handling and packing

- Fungi, bacteria
- Silverfish and woodbeetles
- Rats and mice

Moths   White ants, etc.   **Pests**

to be able to afford similar conservation steps. As for outdoor art, Bachmann suggests that some of it will simply have to be moved indoors. "As the global environment has changed, acid rain and air pollution have become an issue to the extent that preservation for outdoor sculpture may mean removal from an original site,"[17] he says.

the worst possible place to keep anything valuable,"[21] says New York art appraiser Elin Lake Ewald. The magazine *Art News* also reported the case of a seventeenth-century Dutch portrait of a figure whose white shirt had yellowed. When questioned by the conservator they hired, the owners of the painting admitted to trying to clean the portrait with dish detergent.

Preventive Care

Although there are many reasons good art goes bad, Bachmann of the Smithsonian says that proper preventive care can go a long way toward preserving art and ensuring that it would need just a minimum of restoration work. He says, "The emphasis in conservation today is on prevention of deterioration through control of the environment, in climate, storage, and on exhibition."[22]

Preventive care can be as simple as keeping a frisky dog on a leash so the animal does not chew through a painting. Preventive care can also be quite complicated: It may mean displaying a valuable painting in a sealed chamber in which the temperature and humidity are controlled to arrest the deterioration of the pigments or canvas. Preventive care can also include convincing leaders of government and industry to clean up the air—a solution that would improve the health not only of art but of people as well.

How Much Restoration Is Too Much?

In 1820 a farmer on the Greek island of Milo discovered a cave in his field. When the farmer explored the cave he found an unusual marble statue of a woman, obviously carved in ancient times. The statue was heavily damaged; most significantly, it was missing its arms. Despite the damage, the statue was soon purchased by a French diplomat, the Marquis de Rivière, who presented it as a gift to King Louis XVIII. The king ordered the statue repaired, but conservators elected not to fashion new arms for the sculpture. The statue went on display in the Louvre. Today, the *Venus de Milo* is one of the most famous sculptures in the world.

The fact that the *Venus* is still missing its arms has done nothing to detract from its artistic and historical value. In 1895 German archaeologist and historian Adolf Furtwängler submitted sketches to the Louvre in which he proposed to add arms to the *Venus;* according to Furtwängler's plan, one hand would hold an apple, the arm resting on a pedestal, while the other hand would touch the statue's thigh. Furtwängler did base his plan on some evidence—remnants of the statue found in the farmer's cave included a hand clutching an apple—but there was little other proof that would support Furtwängler's notion

Crowds admire the *Venus de Milo* statue in the Louvre.

of how the replacement arms should be fashioned. Brooklyn College art professor Rachel Kousser, who has made a study of the *Venus,* says Furtwängler's idea "was the most plausible hypothesis, although by no means a certain one."[23] Indeed, officials at the Louvre wisely rejected Furtwängler's plan.

Certainly, when the *Venus* was first uncrated at the Louvre, conservators could have easily fashioned arms for the statue. Their decision to leave the *Venus* as it was found serves as an example of how a piece of art can retain its value even though the conservation does not return it to its original form. Conservators are always mindful of the point at which to stop so their efforts do not intrude on the work of the original artist.

More than a Touch-up

Furtwängler's idea for the *Venus de Milo*'s arms was nothing more than an educated guess as to how the arms may have appeared when the statue was carved centuries ago. Historians have concluded that the *Venus* was fashioned between 200 and 100 B.C., but the identity of the sculptor remains unknown. No other evidence exists that would suggest how the original arms were positioned. Therefore, adding arms to the *Venus* without having a notion of how they may have looked was unthinkable to the Louvre conservators.

Conservators are often confronted with repairing pieces of art that have sustained so much damage they need more than a mere touch-up. In the case of paintings, most conservation efforts do result in some degree of repainting. Conservators know there is a fine line between adding a minimal amount of paint to a damaged painting and "overpainting"—applying too much paint, a practice that could dominate the old work and destroy the aesthetic quality of the image that the original artist intended. Says noted conservator Knut Nicolaus, "In the course of being retouched, pictures have been 'completed' and 'beautified' according to the tastes of the time. In the process, without any regard for the original, large and important parts of the painting would be overpainted."[24]

First, the conservator has to decide whether it is worth the effort to retouch. If significant portions of the image have been lost, the conservator may decide to do nothing at all. Any

ADOLF FURTWÄNGLER

Adolf Furtwängler, who proposed restoring the arms to the *Venus de Milo*, was an archaeologist and art historian who was regarded as one of the world's leading experts on ancient Greek art and artifacts. Born in Breisgau, Germany, in 1853, Furtwängler developed a system for categorizing tiny shards of pottery unearthed during archaeological digs. Prior to Furtwängler's work, such shards had prompted little interest among archaeologists, but Furtwängler proved they could make valuable contributions to reconstructing ancient Greek pottery.

Furtwängler's interest in the *Venus de Milo* went further than his proposal to reconstruct the statue's arms. Furtwängler involved himself in an ownership dispute over the statue. Although the statue had been displayed for years in the Louvre in Paris, in the 1890s the German government suggested that it was the rightful owner of the *Venus*. Furtwängler's study of the statue suggested that it had originally been displayed in the civic gymnasium on the island of Milo near where the *Venus* had been discovered. Crown Prince Ludwig I of Bavaria purchased the ruins of the gymnasium in 1817, prompting the German government to argue that the *Venus* had been part of the ruins. The French government ignored Germany's demand, and eventually the furor was forgotten.

Furtwängler died in 1907. Atop his tomb sits a replica of a sphinx he unearthed on the Greek island of Aegina.

replication of the original image that the conservator would create would be more of the conservator's work than that of the original artist. In such cases, modern conservators usually decide to end the restoration work after the painting has undergone the preliminary repair stages. The image is not complete but the painting's deterioration has been arrested. Whatever historical or artistic value that may remain in the image has been preserved. Nicolaus suggests that retouching is an "esthetic luxury,"[25] meaning that the retouching itself does nothing to preserve the original other than helping people see the same vision the artist saw when painting the original image. If the retouching is done poorly, not only will it shed a poor light on the original image, but the misuse of the paint can start the deterioration process all over again. Says David Bomford of the National Gallery of Art in London:

> Restoration has to balance two conflicting requirements—those of legibility and authenticity. On the one hand, an observer wishes to see a composition uninterrupted by damage and loss; but, on the other, it is necessary to know which parts are original paint and

Leonardo da Vinci's wall painting *The Last Supper* is shown here before major restoration was completed in 1999.

which are not. . . . All restoration is a compromise, attempting to diminish the impact of disruptive losses while allowing a painting to appear gracefully old.[26]

Bomford adds that there are certain aspects of a painting's deterioration that the public should find acceptable. For example, simply because a painting is suffering from craquelure does not necessarily mean the cracks should be filled in and touched up. "We expect an old paint film to be cracked and it is not usually disturbing,"[27] he says.

Replicating the Image

Bomford calls the repainting phase of the project "deceptive reconstruction,"[28] meaning that the replicated image is meant to deceive the viewer into believing that the painting has remained in pristine condition since the day it was taken off the artist's easel—perhaps half a millennium ago—and that not a single flake of paint has been lost.

To replicate the image, the conservator will first search for a record of the missing portion. If the painting is hundreds of years old, all records of the original image may have been lost.

After its twenty-one-year restoration process, *The Last Supper* is infused with brighter colors and tones and sharper detail.

Artists' sketches, such as this perspective study of animals and human figures by Leonardo da Vinci, can aid conservators in restoration.

In many cases, though, there remains some record of the original. Perhaps the artist left behind sketches, or an engraving of the original image was published in an old book.

If a record of the lost image is unavailable, the conservator turns next to similar works by the same artist. By studying the artist's other paintings, the conservator can gain a sense and feel for how the artist might have painted a tree or a horse's tail or the hilly background of a landscape. At the National Gallery in London, conservators tackled a work titled *Jesus Opens the Eyes of a Man Born Blind*, painted in 1311 by Italian artist Duccio di Buoninsegna. The painting included three panels of images, each of which showed the face of the blind man. In the final panel, the paint on the man's face had flaked off, obliterating the final dramatic scene in which the man gains his vision. The National Gallery's conservators were able to replicate the man's face because it was clearly visible in the first two panels of the painting.

However, if other sources that depict the lost image are unavailable, then it is up to the conservator to replicate the missing portion of the painting. This step takes a considerable amount of artistic talent; a conservator who does not feel up to the task may hire a skilled artist to complete the painting. The restorer may need to hire and pose a model so that a missing portion of a hand or foot can be painted onto the original. Some artists pose models and photograph them, then work from the photograph. The photograph can be enlarged to the exact size needed for the missing portion of the original painting. A tracing is made of the photograph, then transferred to the canvas, so that the artist can work from the sketch on the surface of the painting.

Striking a Compromise

There is no firm rule that guides the conservator in knowing how much repainting is required or at what point the image becomes overpainted: That decision must be made individually for each painting. In the case of the Sistine Chapel, which features some three hundred figures painted on nearly 6,000 square feet (558 sq. m) of ceiling space, the modern-day conservators found themselves making those decisions on a regular basis.

Unlike the conservators at the Louvre who had few resources on which to draw when restoring the *Venus de Milo*, the Sistine Chapel conservators had access to a large store of records that indicated how Michelangelo painted the original images. Indeed, many of the artist's original sketches for the frescoes still exist. In some cases, the figures in the sketches did not match the images in the frescoes—tiny details were different, such as missing curls of hair adorning the heads of the figures. Using the sketches as a guide, the conservators looked more closely at the frescoes. Occasionally, they found that Michelangelo's original details had been overpainted by past conservators. By using Michelangelo's sketches, they were able to remove the work of the past conservators, revealing the image as the artist truly intended.

That was not always possible. Sometimes, conservators had to strike a compromise between improving the appearance of the frescoes while maintaining a measure of the ceiling's history. For example, when conservators uncovered a crudely painted

Conservators observe a fine line between touching up an image and overpainting—applying so much new paint that the artist's original work is altered. English conservator Ian McClure recalls one painting in which past restorers had overpainted so much that the original image was dramatically changed.

The artwork was a portrait of England's Prince Henry, who lived from 1594 to 1612. Painted in 1610 by Robert Peake, the portrait depicted the prince riding a prancing horse. To begin restoration of the image, conservators studied a small chip of paint under a microscope. The microscopic view led them to the discovery that five separate coats of paint had been added to the original image. Stripping off the additional layers revealed a second image on the canvas: a winged Father Time trailing behind the prince.

Says McClure, "People often expect the cleaning of a painting to lead to an unexpected discovery of some kind. This is in fact quite rare . . . but sometimes the conservator does stumble on an extraordinary find, and the rediscovery of the original composition of the great equestrian portrait of Henry Frederick, Prince of Wales . . . was one of these rare occurrences."

During examination of this portrait of England's Prince Henry, conservators discovered a second image underneath several layers of paint.

Ian McClure, "*Henry, Prince of Wales on Horseback* by Robert Peake the Elder," in *The Art of the Conservator*, ed. Andrew Oddy. Washington: Smithsonian Institution Press, 1992, p. 59.

portion of a scene from Genesis—a fresco portraying the left hand of God—they could not believe that Michelangelo would do such shoddy work. After researching the mystery, the conservators learned that the portion of the fresco in question had broken off the ceiling in the mid-sixteenth century. Artist Domenico Carnevali was called in to fix the damage. Carnevali replastered the ceiling and repainted the hand, but his work was poorly executed. After much deliberation, the Sistine conservators elected to leave the hand painted by Carnevali in the fresco, albeit with a touchup. They reasoned that Carnevali's work, no matter how shoddy, was still a part of the ceiling's history.

Computer images help in restoring the Sistine Chapel frescoes. Restoration can be a delicate process.

Going Too Far?

Nevertheless, in other cases conservators have been criticized for going too far. Some critics have thoroughly denounced the whole Sistine restoration project, arguing that the conservators intruded too far into Michelangelo's original work.

When the restoration of the Sistine Chapel was completed, the conservators unveiled a spectrum of incandescent colors that nobody expected. Once all the old fat-based glue was removed, the ceiling glimmered with bright hues of yellow, blue, orange, red, green, and dozens of other colors. To some critics, the colors were too bright. Art historians questioned whether Michelangelo worked in colors that were so radiant. Comparing the Sistine Chapel to his other work, they found little resemblance.

Critics of the Sistine restoration based their attack on how the conservators treated the two layers of paint that were found beneath the old varnish. The first layer of paint applied to the ceiling is known as the *buon fresco*, or "purest," layer. This is the layer of paint that is absorbed by the plaster in the ceiling. For many frescoes, a *secco*, or "second," layer is also applied. Typically, *secco* layers are applied before the *buon fresco* layer is dry. There are many reasons an artist might want to apply the *secco* layer. For example, since the *buon fresco* layer is permanent, it gives the artist no room for error. By applying a *secco* layer, the artist can correct little mistakes or even add features to the

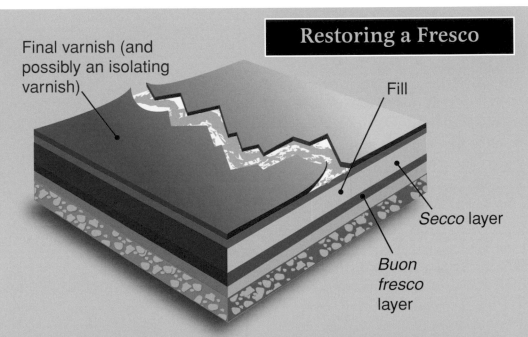

Restoring a Fresco

Final varnish (and possibly an isolating varnish)

Fill

Secco layer

Buon fresco layer

When the Sistine Chapel underwent restoration, two different layers of paint existed, the bottom or *buon fresco* layer, and the top, or *secco* layer. In areas where the original layer had cracked, conservators applied a fill, and then lightly retouched it with paint. The *secco* layer was totally removed, since the paint had been mixed with a fat-based adhesive, which had darkened with age. This alteration of Michelangelo's work was one of the chief criticisms of the project.

scene. The *secco* layer can also be used to alter the color tone of the first layer, usually by making it darker.

To enable the *secco* layer to bond to the *buon fresco* layer, an adhesive must be mixed into the pigment. In Michelangelo's day, the adhesive was typically a fat-based glue or a mixture of egg yolks and oil. Because these ingredients are organic in nature they will darken and harden over the years. "*Secco* work, which lies on the surface, is particularly prone to injury by harsh cleaning, fungal growth and internal composition," says art history professor James Beck. "It can harden, darken and crack, or flake from the plaster surface."[29]

Beck has argued that it was Michelangelo who painted the *secco* layer onto the frescoes and that, therefore, the artist was well aware that the frescoes would dull over time. Beck also suggests that the shades applied by Michelangelo were on the dark side to begin with. He believes that Michelangelo preferred dark hues, which explains why the ceiling of the Sistine Chapel prior to its restoration matched the artist's other paintings. What is more, Beck argues, there is evidence to suggest that the layer of fat-based glue was applied as part of the *secco* layer by Michelangelo himself and not by a conservator working decades later. Therefore, Beck says, when the modern conservators stripped off the layer of glue, they stripped off Michelangelo's original work. He asks, "Did Michelangelo modify and embellish his frescoes after the application of the *buon fresco* layer with traditional *secco* media such as . . . glue-based painting, or not? If he did, then the restorers' removal not just of dirt but of everything down to the frescoed plaster has falsified his work and partly destroyed one of the greatest masterpieces of Western art."[30] Beck and other critics led a campaign to halt restoration of the Sistine Chapel ceiling, but the Vatican refused to stop the project.

Uncovering New Truths

Some public campaigns to halt a restoration have been successful. In 2001, the Uffizi Gallery in Florence, Italy, announced plans to restore a painting by Leonardo da Vinci titled *The Adoration of the Magi.* The painting, which da Vinci started in 1481 but never finished, depicts the three kings visiting the Virgin Mary after the birth of Jesus. Clearly, the painting is unfinished—the canvas includes bare spots. The *Adoration* hung in the Uffizi Gallery for more than three hundred years, picking up a coat of grime and sustaining other damage. For example, the *Adoration* is painted on ten wooden panels joined side by side. Gallery officials discovered the panels separating and concluded that the warps were caused by humidity generated by the breath of hundreds of thousands of visitors leaning too close to get a better look. Also, conservators discovered that many coats of fat-based varnish had been slathered across the *Adoration*, darkening the image and leaving a dull tone. In fact, in some places the finish was so dull it

The Uffizi Gallery in Florence opted to do only minor repairs on Leonardo da Vinci's unfinished painting *The Adoration of the Magi* (pictured).

obliterated features that had been painted by da Vinci. Says Uffizi director Annamaria Petrioli Tofani, "These prevent us from appreciating the real Leonardo. It is as if we were reading a poem where there were two words, then one lacking, two words, then one lacking."[31]

By now, Beck had formed ArtWatch International, an organization of art historians who advocate a conservative approach to art conservation. ArtWatch submitted a petition to Uffizi officials signed by thirty art scholars arguing that the *Adoration* was too fragile a painting to undergo a radical cleaning. Says Beck, "If there is a conservation emergency, if the paint is falling off, if there are termites, fine. But if there is no real loss, why run the risk?"[32]

The Uffizi did not automatically dismiss ArtWatch's concerns. The gallery called in an independent expert, who assessed the painting and sided with ArtWatch. "Based on what we found, I would rule out any major work at this point,"[33] said the independent art diagnostician, Maurizio Seracini.

In fact, when Seracini examined the *Adoration*, he learned new truths about da Vinci's work. Using the scientific techniques of the conservator, including X-ray imaging and infrared photography, Seracini was able to uncover sketches beneath the paint that showed a group of men rebuilding a stone structure behind the Virgin Mary. The discovery of the image led Seracini as well as art historians to suggest that da Vinci may have intended to tell more than just a religious story in the *Adoration*. Indeed, da Vinci may have been making the statement that the European world was emerging from the Middle Ages and was about to be rebuilt. Says da Vinci scholar Carlo Pedretti, "This new interpretation is well accepted now. . . . What [Seracini] has found recently gives us perfect knowledge of the painting. It's an extraordinary thing that's underneath here."[34]

Minor Repairs Instead

The *Adoration* did undergo some minor repairs to close the gaps between the wood panels. Nevertheless, da Vinci's unfinished

For more than two hundred years, this painting of icebergs (right) was hidden under a later tropical painting by the same artist (left). Art restoration technology using X-rays revealed the existence of the iceberg painting.

work went back on the gallery wall in virtually the same condition in which it had come down, with the same dull finish and muted colors.

The effort to halt the restoration of the *Adoration* shows how art conservation can uncover new truths about an artist's work even when the actual restoration of the painting is minor. If ArtWatch had never launched the campaign to halt the restoration, it is likely the Uffizi would never have sought the independent analysis that uncovered the hidden sketches beneath da Vinci's work.

Opposing Viewpoints

The debate over how much conservation is too much is likely to continue. Art is, after all, a form of expression in which opposing viewpoints are the norm. Two people standing in front of a painting may find themselves in total disagreement about its artistic qualities. That applies to restored paintings as well. One person standing beneath the ceiling of the Sistine Chapel may appreciate the incandescent colors uncovered during the last restoration of Michelangelo's frescoes. Another person may long to see the images as they were in the sixteenth century—dark and muted beneath the *secco* layer.

Art in Times of Crisis

On September 11, 2001, art valued at an estimated $100 million was destroyed in the collapse of the twin towers of the World Trade Center in New York City. Valuable paintings that hung in the headquarters of some of the city's largest corporations were among the pieces lost in the terrorist attack, including a painting by Roy Lichtenstein, one of the pioneers of abstract art. Some of the city's most avant-garde sculpture was also destroyed, including a 25-foot [7.6m] red steel abstract by Alexander Calder titled *Bent Propeller* and a carved wood wall hanging by Louise Nevelson titled *Sky Gate New York*. Crushed beneath tons of rubble at ground zero, that art is lost forever. "It's like losing a family member,"[35] says Calder's grandson, Alexander Rower.

Art is often caught in the crossfire of war or left behind during such natural disasters as hurricanes, floods, and earthquakes. Once the shooting stops or the flood waters recede, museum officials, gallery owners, and private collectors return to find that priceless art has sustained heavy damage. Some of it is beyond repair, but a large proportion is surprisingly salvageable. Even in the rubble of the World Trade Center, one piece of art—a sculpture by Fritz Koenig titled *The Sphere*—

Alexander Calder's metal sculpture *Bent Propeller* was destroyed in the terrorist attacks of September 11, 2001.

was unearthed, damaged but repairable. In today's world, art conservators are often called in under the most devastating of circumstances to save art damaged by war, fire, and flood.

Looting Iraq's National Treasures

In the days immediately following the invasion of Iraq on April 5, 2003, chaos ruled the capital city of Baghdad. As American troops fought to establish order, their goals included defeating the troops loyal to dictator Saddam Hussein and providing the population of the beleaguered city with the basic necessities of life—food, electric power, and running water, among them. Saving priceless works of art and important antiquities was not a priority.

The chief victim of this neglect was the Iraq Museum in Baghdad, an institution in the city for more than eighty years. Thieves and vandals broke into the museum and stole or damaged some fifteen thousand works of art and antiquities, some of which were more than seventy-five hundred years old. Iraq sits in the heart of the Middle East crescent formerly known as Mesopotamia; its borders include the ancient city of Babylon, regarded as the birthplace of civilization. Iraq has thus been the natural depository for thousands of pieces of ancient art and antiquities that can be found in no other place on the planet. Recalls Iraq Museum director Donny George Youkahanna,

> The looters broke through the main museum galleries and the store rooms, stealing and destroying everything they could get their hands on. In many cases, what they could not take they smashed and destroyed, including the head of a terra-cotta lion from . . . the Old Babylonian period around 1800 B.C., and Roman statues found in the city of Hatra, from the first century B.C.[36]

The thousands of pieces stolen from the museum included sculptures depicting ancient gods and mortals; vases, pots, and other ceramics, including some whose bright colors managed

Looters stole thousands of pieces of priceless artwork from the Iraqi National Museum (pictured).

IN THE DANGER ZONE

Many pieces of Iraqi art were preserved thanks to the efforts of heroic officials at the Iraq Museum. During the months following the 2003 American invasion, museum director Donny George Youkahanna and three other officials remained at their posts to protect the pieces remaining in the looted museum and salvage what they could from the exhibits that had been smashed by the looters. Part of their task was to document the thefts and damage so the world could be alerted to the wanton looting of the national treasures. They chronicled the loss in a book, *The Looting of the Iraq Museum.* To help prepare the book, they were joined by writer-photographer Micah Garen and an interpreter, Amir Doshe.

They were not armed nor were they protected by troops. In fact, in 2004 Garen and Doshe were kidnapped by insurgents. Fortunately, friends in Iraq interceded on their behalf. They were released unharmed on the orders of Muqtada al-Sadr, the Islamic cleric who exercises an enormous amount of influence in the country.

Artwork smashed by looters covers the floor of Iraq's national museum in Baghdad.

to survive thousands of years after they were cast; and plaques carved from ivory depicting wild animals that roamed the Mesopotamian landscape. Thieves also carried off solid gold relics, including bowls and jewelry found by archaeologists near the Iraqi city of Mosul, as well as Babylonian coins depicting the image of the Macedonian conqueror known as Alexander the Great.

Other institutions were also victimized. About fifteen hundred paintings and sculptures were stolen from the Baghdad Museum of Fine Arts. Hundreds of thousands of books were stolen from the Iraq National Library and burned. Soon after the invasion, United Nations official Mounir Bouchenaki toured the damaged institutions, saying, "This is a real cultural disaster, and we will have to redo everything from scratch in rebuilding these cultural institutions."[37]

Conservation Triumph

About four thousand pieces of the looted art and antiquities were recovered in Iraq and returned to the Iraq Museum, either by Iraqi police or American troops. One of the returned relics was a thirty-two-hundred-year-old marble sculpture known as the *Lady of Warka*, which depicts the head of a young woman. Another two thousand pieces were found in other Arab countries or in Europe or the United States. They had been smuggled out of Iraq and sold to collectors. Still, thousands of pieces remain missing.

As for the art and antiquities that were returned to the museum, many of them are in damaged condition. Thanks to an effort sponsored by art and antiquities conservation groups in Italy, the United States, and other countries, steps are now being taken to restore the damaged pieces. Private foundations have contributed to the establishment of a new state-of-the-art conservation laboratory at the Iraq Museum. One of the first triumphs of the conservation lab was the restoration of the *Uruk Vase*, a fifty-two-hundred-year-old relic whose surface features carvings depicting life in ancient Iraq as well as images of Mesopotamian gods. The vase was stolen from the museum, then returned anonymously in about a half-dozen pieces. The shards were pieced together and glued in the museum's new conservation lab; today, the cracks are evident but the relic is once again intact.

DAMAGING BABYLON

Sometimes, art and antiquities are damaged not by looters or enemy soldiers, but by the liberators. During the Iraq War, American troops established a helicopter base near an archaeological dig centered in the ancient city of Babylon. Soon, it became apparent that the daily flights made by the heavy aircraft were damaging the relics. Vibrations from the choppers rattled the walls, while the rotors propelled dust and debris into the fragile bricks used to build the city more than eight thousand years ago.

Columbia University art history and archaeology professor Zainab Bahrani was a witness to the damage. She says,

> Between May and August 2004, the wall of the Temple of Nabu and the roof of the Temple of Ninmah, both of the sixth century B.C., collapsed as a result of the movement of helicopters. Nearby, heavy machines and vehicles stand parked on the remains of a Greek theater from the era of Alexander of Macedon. The minister of culture has asked for the removal of military bases from all archaeological sites, but none has yet been relocated.

When Bahrani asked for the helicopters to be removed, military officials told her that the aircraft were too important for the security of the American troops.

Zainab Bahrani, "The Fall of Babylon," in *The Looting of the Iraq Museum, Baghdad: The Lost Legacy of Ancient Mesopotamia.* Milbry Polk and Angela M.H. Schuster, eds. New York: Harry N. Abrams, 2005, pp. 214–16.

Hurricane Katrina

Wars on the scale of the Iraq invasion are rare, but hurricanes, fires, and floods are a fact of life in America and around the world. Museums and galleries are often located in the path of devastation. Museums along the American Gulf Coast were hit hard in the summer of 2005 due to the devastation caused by Hurricane Katrina. The city of Biloxi, Mississippi, serves as an example. Biloxi's economy was built largely on the shrimp industry. To celebrate the hardworking shrimp boat crews, local sculptor Harry Reeks fashioned the bronze statue *Golden Fisherman*, which depicts a shrimp boat crewman casting a net. For years, *Golden Fisherman* stood on a pedestal in Point Cadet Plaza, a public park along the Gulf Coast. Hurricane Katrina blew *Golden Fisherman* off the pedestal, ripping the statue apart at the ankles.

When the storm made landfall, it devastated Biloxi. Thousands of homes were damaged or destroyed, leaving many residents homcless. Streets were submerged under the flood; utilities such as water, sewage, and electrical service were damaged. Eventually, the storm blew past two important Biloxi cultural institutions—the Ohr-O'Keefe Museum of Art and the home and library of Confederate president Jefferson Davis, which is known as Beauvoir.

The Ohr-O'Keefe Museum houses a collection of ceramics fashioned by the late artist George Ohr, a truly eccentric local figure known as the Mad Potter of Biloxi. The curators of

Beauvoir, the house of Confederate president Jefferson Davis in Biloxi, Mississippi, sustained heavy damage from Hurricane Katrina in 2005.

the Ohr-O'Keefe Museum had heeded the warnings of the hurricane. They packed up the pottery and shipped it to a safe location before the storm hit the region. That turned out to be a wise decision. The museum is housed in five buildings on the Ohr-O'Keefe property, and all of them suffered some degree of damage. The newest building, which was designed to house African American art, was still unfinished. It was totally destroyed when winds from Katrina lifted a nearby casino boat out of the water and slammed it into the building.

Beauvoir—the French word means "beautiful view"—also suffered greatly in the storm. The property included a complex of seven buildings, some of which housed an extensive collection of pre–Civil War art. Five of the seven buildings were destroyed by the storm while the two surviving buildings sustained heavy wind and water damage. Indeed, Beauvoir was hit by a 30-foot (9m) wall of water that blew across the two-lane highway separating the estate from the Biloxi beach. Debris from the complex was spread across a 55-acre (22ha) tract surrounding the property. Once the floodwaters subsided, workers found remnants from the buildings mired in mud hundreds of yards away. Some of the paintings and Davis family artifacts were coated with mud for weeks. Asked to describe his reaction to the damage, Beauvoir curator Patrick Hotard responded, "Devastated. It's a feeling of emptiness."[38]

Caked in Mud

Elsewhere along the Gulf Coast, many museums suffered similar damage. In Louisiana, the New Orleans Museum of Art sustained some damage from the storm—windows were blown out and utilities were interrupted, placing some of the climate-controlled exhibits at risk but leaving them largely intact. Outside, though, artist Kenneth Snelson's 45-foot-tall (14m) steel sculpture titled *Virlane Tower* was severely twisted by the storm. New Orleans photographer Herman Leonard, who spent a lifetime chronicling the city's jazz community, lost most of his prints when his home and studio were flooded with water. Luckily, the negatives had been moved to another location

HERMAN LEONARD

$\mathcal{A}$n artist whose work was devastated by Hurricane Katrina is Herman Leonard, whose career as a photographer spans more than sixty years. He is known mostly for his portraits of jazz greats, such as Dizzy Gillespie, Charlie Parker, and Dexter Gordon.

After serving in World War II, Leonard earned a degree from Ohio University, then served for a year as an apprentice to famed portrait photographer Yousuf Karsh. Leonard then opened his own photography studio. He traveled often, taking photographic assignments across the globe. A true fan of jazz music, Leonard never missed an opportunity to photograph the colorful musicians of jazz. His portraits have been displayed in the Smithsonian Institution and other important museums.

Leonard's New Orleans home and studio and archive of prints were destroyed by Hurricane Katrina. Although the negatives were saved, his agent and assistant, Jennifer Bagert, explains that no two prints made from the same negative are exactly alike and it may be difficult to duplicate the originals. She says, "Herman is one of the last master photographers who is also a master printer. I think he'll print till the day he dies because it gives him great pleasure. But it will be difficult to recreate everything that was lost. It's difficult to recreate what he does with a photograph, anyway. We take notes, we watch. You try to recreate the *Mona Lisa*, but it won't have the same magic."

Jazz legend Ella Fitzgerald performs in front of Duke Ellington in this 1948 photo by Herman Leonard. Many of Leonard's photographs were destroyed by Hurricane Katrina.

Quoted in Geoff Gehman, "After Katrina, Famed Artist Tries to Right His Life," *Allentown Morning Call*, September 18, 2005.

for safekeeping. Still, shortly after the storm the photographer's agent and assistant, Jennifer Bagert, said, "There are stacks and stacks of these photos. They are still wet. . . . The second you peel the plastic off, the image is gone. He's 82 and no one prints like he does. There's this impulse to try and save everything. You just have to let it go."[39]

In Ocean Springs, Mississippi, much of the work of painter and sculptor Walter Anderson was ruined when the late artist's home was leveled by the storm. Anderson, whose work has been featured in the Smithsonian Institution and other major museums, was something of an eccentric: He often lived outdoors, and he preferred to paint on tiny Horn Island in the Gulf of Mexico, where he died in 1965. Anderson's family thought they had taken the necessary steps to protect his work. Hundreds of paintings and sculptures had been housed in a steel, wood, and concrete vault built on the property. Nevertheless, the storm waters found their way into the vault. After looking over Anderson's art, most of which was soaked in water or caked in mud, his son John Anderson said, "A lot of this can be dealt with, with proper conservation. Some things can be done. Some things cannot be done."[40]

A ceiling and walls decorated by artist Walter Anderson at a community center in Ocean Springs, Mississippi, were ruined by Hurricane Katrina.

In fact, conservators can clean paintings and other works of art that have been damaged by floodwaters and mud. Conservators first tilt the painting to drain off excess water. If the paint on the canvas is intact, conservators use blotting paper to lift off the mud. After allowing the surface to dry, the conservator will then lightly brush off the remaining dirt or clean the surface with distilled water or solvents that will not harm the paint. Art conservators also use lasers to burn dried mud off the surface of a painting.

If the water and mud have damaged the surface of the painting, causing the paint to flake, the process becomes much more delicate. The conservator will clean the painting as much as possible, then reattach the flaking paint using glue and Japan paper. The process is long and tedious: The surface around each piece of flaked paint needs to be cleaned with handheld swabs. The flakes will then be individually glued back onto the canvas.

Working in Moon Suits

The damage suffered by the Anderson paintings shows just how delicate storm-damaged art can be, prompting conservators to use caution when handling art that has been damaged by natural catastrophes. The art is very fragile because soaking in water for a lengthy period of time can loosen paint and corrode metals. Conservators must also be cautious about their own health when entering a storm-damaged scene. For example, sewage pipes may have burst, flooding the area with bacteria that could cause hepatitis and other diseases. Conservators may need immunization shots before venturing into the storm zone. Mold spores caused by dampness can cause health problems. Tetanus vaccines may also be necessary because sharp objects that can pierce rubber boots may be lurking underwater or stuck in mud.

Conservators may need protective gear when going into the storm zone. Conservator Chris Stavroudis says he has worn goggles, rubber gloves, and boots—even hip waders—when the water level has been high. Stavroudis has also used a respirator, which he says is important for conservators who suffer from asthma or a similar condition.

Sometimes, complete body protection is necessary. Workers who clean up hazardous waste sites wear full-body containment suits called moon suits, because they resemble the spacesuits worn by astronauts. Occasionally, conservators have found it necessary to don the suits, which are sewn from a material composed of plastic fibers. Stavroudis recalls cleaning a mural and stained-glass window that had been contaminated in a hazardous waste incident:

> So we entered the work area. Completely covered. No drinks or water. No potty breaks. No mopping the sweat from our brows (or rather getting it off my nose as it came dripping down my face—of course this all happened in the hottest week of the summer). . . .
>
> This is a very odd experience. Communication is difficult. It's somewhat difficult to climb scaffolding in this get-up. It is easy to get overheated, disoriented, and to feel claustrophobic. You might even face a bit of a panic attack the first time you enter a site dressed like this.[41]

Saving Winnie Davis

The conservators who helped rescue the paintings and artifacts from Beauvoir did not have to wear moon suits. Still, they faced the lengthy process of finding the lost art work scattered around the estate and then retrieving the pieces and packaging them for shipment to a conservation lab. After the hurricane, the conservation lab at the Winterthur Museum in Delaware along with conservation students from the University of Delaware accepted the task of repairing the Beauvoir paintings and other artifacts.

One of the paintings that desperately needed treatment depicted Winnie Davis, the youngest daughter of Jefferson Davis. The painting, which measures 42 by 67 inches (107 by 170cm), was painted in 1892. It hung above the mantel in the

Davis home for more than one hundred years. After the storm waters subsided, museum officials realized that the flood had reached its high-water mark in the house near the first-floor ceiling—meaning that the portrait of Winnie Davis had spent several days submerged. When the conservators in Delaware unpacked it from its crate, they found the canvas had actually sagged—an alarming condition that could cause the paint to fall off. The portrait was slathered in mud, with debris, including mud, sand, and plaster, wedged between the canvas and the frame. At the Winterthur, conservators went to work on the portrait to glue down the curling paint and fill the cracks caused when the water dried.

A portrait of Jefferson Davis's daughter Winnie (pictured) was submerged in floodwaters in New Orleans during Katrina but conservators salvaged the painting.

Given the number of paintings and other pieces of art damaged by Hurricane Katrina as well as other recent natural disasters, conservators have a lot of work ahead of them. Still, the enthusiasm to fix what is broken is there. Soon after the floodwaters in Biloxi subsided, city officials announced a campaign to put *Golden Fisherman* back on its pedestal.

Campaigning for Public Art

With all that needs to be done to restore homes and businesses along the Gulf Coast, the effort by Biloxi to restore *Golden Fisherman* represents a considerable sacrifice by the local residents and merchants who have contributed to the campaign. Elsewhere, communities with far fewer problems have not been quite as ready to preserve and restore the public art that graces their parks and squares. Indeed, thousands of statues and other examples of public art in America are slowly deteriorating from neglect because cash-strapped governments are hesitant to save them. Sometimes, private citizens must step in to save endangered works of art.

Saving Public Art

There are more than thirty-two thousand public sculptures in the United States and, according to a study done in the 1990s, more than half of them are suffering from some degree of deterioration. They range from a poison ivy–covered bust of William Shakespeare in Tennessee to Mount Rushmore in South Dakota, where the 60-foot-high (18m) granite likenesses of George Washington, Abraham Lincoln, Thomas Jefferson, and Theodore Roosevelt sat for years under layers of dirt until they were cleaned in 2005.

In the United States, public art is typically owned by city and state governments as well as the federal government. In many cases, the art was donated to a community by a well-meaning benefactor who unfortunately neglected to set aside funds for the upkeep of the gift, so the sculpture sits outdoors exposed to all manner of conditions, including snow, rain, ice, pollution, and vandalism. As a result, the art falls into disrepair, often before the eyes of thousands of people who drive by it every day. Says Gregory Andrews, an architectural historian who assessed the conditions of statues of Nathan Hale and other Revolutionary War heroes located in Connecticut, "The deteriorating condition of sculptures honoring heroes is a real disgrace. These sculptures deserve better."[42]

Some cities do buy their own art. In the 1970s, many communities adopted Percent-for-Art programs in which 1 percent of the construction budget of a new municipal building or park was devoted to obtaining outdoor art for the facility. The problem with the Percent-for-Art programs soon became evident: few of them provided money for the ongoing maintenance of the art. The local governments responsible for the upkeep of the statues are hesitant to devote the money or labor necessary to preserve the pieces. Cash-strapped cities find it difficult to allocate money to maintaining a resource that provides no direct benefit to the taxpayers.

And so it is usually left up to private citizens to save public art. In many cases, the sculpture may define their community, if, for example, the statue in the park was erected in honor of the town's founder or represents a notable achievement in the history of the community. The statuary may be part of a monument to the city's veterans. Usually, citizens must organize on their own, raise money, and hire conservators who face the challenges of restoring art that often provides an identity to a community and, in some cases, the entire nation.

The face of Thomas Jefferson gets a makeover during restoration of the Mount Rushmore sculpture.

Restoring a National Treasure

By the 1980s, it became clear to advocates of art that thousands of public statues in the United States were in serious trouble. If they were made of metals such as bronze, they were likely to be suffering from corrosion. Typically, water seeps into the statue and starts eating away at the metal from the inside. Stone statues fashioned from granite or marble were in disrepair as well, particularly in northern cities. When water seeps into a tiny crack in a piece of stone and then freezes, it will expand the crack. Over a period of years or decades, the fissures created by the constant exposure to rain and ice can become quite deep. Public sculptures that sit atop fountains are even more susceptible to damage; it does not have to be a rainy day for them to be exposed to moisture.

Rain and ice are not always the culprits. Some outdoor sculptures suffer from neglect that cause them to lose their value as public art. Tennessee State Museum official Carolann Haggard recalls an unsuccessful search for a bust of William Shakespeare that was supposed to have been on display at Lookout Mountain National Military Park near Chattanooga. Evidently, the bust was so covered with poison ivy and other vegetation that no one could find it. Adds Susan Nichols, a director of the national program known as Save Outdoor Sculpture!, "I call outdoor sculpture 'orphans of the cultural community.' Outdoor sculpture often suffers from benign neglect, as well as from the environment. We need to become more active and vigilant in caring for them."[43]

Neglect does not just affect obscure sculptures such as the Shakespeare bust on Lookout Mountain. Some important national icons suffer from deterioration because the federal government fails to keep them in repair. The Statue of Liberty serves as an example.

Designed by French sculptor Frédéric-Auguste Bartholdi, the 151-foot (46m), 156-ton (141-m ton) statue was erected on what was formerly known as Bedloe's Island in New York Harbor. It arrived at the island in 1885 in 214 crates (it took longshoremen more than two weeks to unload the freighter) and was assembled on the site. The statue itself was a gift to the American people from the French, who intended it as a celebration of democracy, but erecting it in New York Harbor depended on the ability of sponsors in America to raise money. When the fund-raising faltered, New York publisher Joseph Pulitzer used his newspaper to raise the final $100,000—a considerable sum in those days—that was needed to build the 27,000-ton (24,494-m ton) concrete pedestal.

The statue was completed and dedicated in 1886; it instantly became a national treasure, particularly in 1903 after the poem "The New Colossus" by Emma Lazarus was engraved onto a plaque that was installed on the base. Lazarus's stirring words —*Give me your tired, your poor, / Your huddled masses yearning to breathe free . . .*—greeted hundreds of thousands of European immigrants who sailed past the statue on their way to nearby Ellis Island, the immigration center where they hoped to start new lives in America.

From the time it was dedicated, the statue fell under the care of a number of obscure federal agencies; something called the United States Lighthouse Board was the first caretaker. In 1933

In 1883 workmen in France hammer sheets of copper for the construction of the Statue of Liberty. The statue's left arm and shoulder are visible.

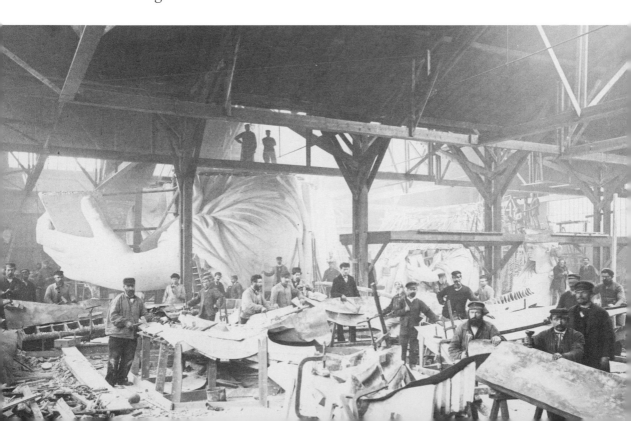

The artist who designed and oversaw construction of the Statue of Liberty was Frédéric-Auguste Bartholdi, who was born in 1834 in Colmar, a city in the Alsace region of France. During the Franco-Prussian War of 1870, Alsace became part of Germany. The experience of losing his home to an aggressive foreign power made Bartholdi appreciate the cause of democracy and helped inspire his design for the statue.

He was also inspired by the 76-foot (23m) statue of St. Charles Borromeo, a sixteenth-century archbishop, which Bartholdi saw while on a visit to Venice, Italy, in 1869. The statue was constructed of a copper skin placed over a steel framework. To duplicate the design for the Statue of Liberty, Bartholdi called on the assistance of engineer Alexandre Gustav Eiffel, a noted designer of railroad bridges. After completing his work on the Statue of Liberty, Eiffel designed Paris's most famous landmark, the 900-foot (275m) Eiffel Tower.

Bartholdi worked on the Statue of Liberty for fifteen years. After completing the statue, he returned to Paris, where he maintained a busy sculpture studio. He died in 1904.

the National Park Service took over ownership of the statue. Three years later, the agency sponsored a minor restoration that probably did more harm than good. By then, some of the copper skin was peeling off the frame; restorers reattached the copper sheets by using screws rather than rivets, leaving room for water to seep into the screw holes. To seal the screw holes, restorers painted over them on the interior surface of the statue. Instead of adequately sealing the screw holes, the paint masked corrosion that was forming underneath. Ironically, Bartholdi had suggested that if future conservators would use the same techniques he employed—which they ultimately did not—the statue would be better able to resist corrosion. Wrote Bartholdi, "In regard to the preservation of the work, since all the elements of its construction are everywhere visible on the inside in all their details, it will be easily kept in good condition."[44]

Following that modest and largely ineffective restoration, the National Park Service continued to provide routine maintenance, but it was not enough. Decades of standing tall against the storms and salty air of the Atlantic Ocean took their toll on the statue, further corroding the copper skin and steel framework inside. In time, it became clear that something dramatic had to be done.

A New Torch for the Statue of Liberty

The $87 million cost of restoring the statue was regarded as too steep for the National Park Service to underwrite; indeed, the entire art maintenance budget of the federal government is a mere $1 million a year. In response, a committee of citizens was formed to raise money for the restoration of the statue as well as the renovation of the immigration center on Ellis Island, which the committee intended to turn into a museum. The Statue of Liberty–Ellis Island Centennial Commission turned the task into a national campaign; its chair, automotive industry executive Lee Iacocca, pleaded for donations from the American people. The campaign was an overwhelming success; the statue was restored and the new Ellis Island museum completed in time for a 1986 celebration marking the statue's hundredth anniversary.

Restoration work on the statue lasted two years. During the project, the statue took on a new look—it was completely encased in scaffolding, which allowed the workers access to every inch of the exterior skin. The work on the Statue of Liberty illustrates some of the problems conservators face when restoring public art: frequently, the art is very tall, requiring conservators to work atop scaffolding dozens or even hundreds of feet above the ground.

The Statue of Liberty is covered in scaffolding during its 1984 restoration. Nearly a century of exposure to the elements had corroded the statue.

Restoration of the Statue of Liberty required the skills of more than just art conservators; laborers from the metalworking trades were vital to the project. Architects, scientists, and engineers were called in to produce drawings, schematics, and analyses of the structure as well as solutions to the problems that were uncovered during the restoration. They employed some very sophisticated gadgetry, including an ultrasonic caliper designed to measure the thickness of the skin without coming into contact with the surface. The caliper discovered that the skin generally measures 0.08 inches (2 mm)—about the thickness of a penny. The caliper was employed to determine whether the skin had eroded since it was first attached to the steel skeleton. The device showed that no erosion had occurred, although in some cases holes opened up in the skin due to rust.

Repairing the Skin

With the scaffolding in place, conservators were able to take a very close look at the exterior skin. The skin, fashioned from red copper, had developed a green patina over the decades of exposure to the moist air. The patina is the natural film of oxidation found on metals. Development of the patina was natural and even anticipated by Bartholdi. However, the conservators found corrosion, cracks, and tears around rivet holes. To repair the damage, the old screws and rivets were removed and new rivets installed. To repair the corrosion and tears, the conservators performed what is known as a wolf-mouth assembly. A mold is first created, using the old surface to develop the shape of a replacement piece. The replacement piece is then fashioned in a shop. Next, the damaged piece of skin is cut off. To fit the new piece into place, the edges are cut in a sawtooth pattern, resembling the mouth of a wolf. A similar sawtooth pattern is cut into the edges where the damaged piece was cut off. Then, the new piece is fitted into place, with the two sawtooth edges matching. Finally, the replacement piece is welded to the statue.

Bartholdi's design for the statue's robe provided dozens of crevices—perfect for the construction of birds' nests. A family of birds living in a fold of the Statue of Liberty's robe may have been a touching sight, but after several decades the bird droppings had in many places produced a solid black layer that was eating through the copper skin.

There was considerable structural damage as well; the steel frame holding aloft the torch and flame was in danger of collapse. Over the years, water, bird droppings, and pollutants had seeped into the frame and pooled in a reservoir just below the torch, gradually eating away at the steel and weakening the frame. The deterioration was so severe that the project's conservators elected to completely replace the torch and flame. A new torch and flame was fashioned in a workshop and hoisted into place atop the statue's upraised arm.

Making It Last

Despite the extensive repair work that was needed, given the severe weather that blows through New York Harbor, the fact that the Statue of Liberty survived as well as it has is testament to Bartholdi's vision. Other artists have been far less concerned with the future problems their art may cause its owners. Years after their installations, public art often deteriorates because it is not able to stand up against the climate. If the artists had used materials more appropriate for the climate or location where the sculpture was installed, perhaps the piece would be better able to weather the elements. Says New York sculptor Alan Sonfist, who has accepted a number of commissions to provide public art, "Part of the challenge of creating public art is combining appropriate materials and an artistic vision. If you are putting something in the ground, you have to consider the acidity of the soil. If you are working in a place that is very humid or very dry, you have to know how your materials will interact with that environment."[45]

Today's city governments and museums are working closely with art conservators, asking them to review an artist's proposal for a sculpture before the piece is accepted. In Philadelphia, for example, conservators working with the Fairmount Park Commission, which is responsible for overseeing the city's public park system, have asked artists to alter their designs or construction materials so the sculptures are better able to weather Philadelphia's very hot summers and very cold winters. The charge for the conservators, according to Park Commission assistant director Laura Griffiths, is to "find the most durable materials that still meet the integrity of the artist's idea."[46] In one recent case, sculptor Jody Pinto agreed to alter her statue, *Fingerspan*, to provide for better drainage before it was installed in Fairmount Park.

When restoring public art, part of the conservator's job is to figure out how to prevent future problems. The governments that own public art would prefer not to take a sculpture off its pedestal and spend months as well as tens of thousands of dollars repairing its damage, only to put it back on the same pedestal where it will face the same type of environmental exposure that caused the damage in the first place. Art conservators have the task of finding ways to make the sculpture last longer.

In Scottsdale, Arizona, sculptor Louise Nevelson's outdoor work *Windows to the West* stood in front of the Scottsdale Civic Center since 1973. Scottsdale does not endure harsh winters; nevertheless, by 2003 the abstract steel-plate statue was showing signs of wear. Water had seeped into the steel tubing, causing corrosion. Over the years, the sculpture provided a roost for pigeons, which meant it sustained damage from their droppings. Conservators repaired *Windows to the West* by remaking some of the steel plates in a foundry. To make the statue last longer, "weep" holes were drilled in the base, providing an outlet for rain to escape through the bottom. To discourage pigeons from roosting, extra steel plates were installed on angles in hidden places along the horizontal sections of the work—giving the birds few places where they could perch. Finally, when the statue was reinstalled in front of the Scottsdale Civic Center, its new base was higher, which kept it out of a pool of standing water that would often collect around the statue.

Workers pressure wash statues outside a church in Krakow, Poland. Care and maintenance of public art requires a continual effort.

WHEN PUBLIC ART IS NOT OWNED BY THE PUBLIC

Sometimes, a piece of art becomes so familiar and so much a part of a community that the public claims ownership to it, even though it is not owned by a government or community organization. For more than thirty years, a wall standing in the New York City tavern Costello's has been decorated with original art drawn by cartoonists who stopped in for drinks. Original sketches of Beetle Bailey, Bullwinkle, Spider-Man, Hagar the Horrible, and other characters were drawn onto the wall by the artists who created them.

In 2004, Costello's changed ownership, prompting fears that the new proprietors would tear down the wall. The New York Historical Society, the Museum of the City of New York, and the *New York Daily News* urged the new owners to preserve the comic strip wall during a planned renovation of the tavern. Indeed, during the renovation the wall was covered with plastic sheets that shielded it from dust and debris raised during the construction work.

Jeff Perzan, one of the new owners of the tavern, assured the community that the comic strip wall would remain standing. "Of course we weren't going to tear it down," he said. "It was one of the selling points of the building."

Quoted in Benjamin T. Oderwald and Christine Gibson, "The Faces on the Barroom Wall," *American Heritage*, October 2004, p. 17.

Gloucester Fisherman

Although many successes have been recorded in the drive to save public art, most outdoor sculpture continues to deteriorate. The Save Outdoor Sculpture! program, which is supported by the Smithsonian Institution and Heritage Preservation, a Washington-based organization that provides art conservation assistance to small communities and museums, conducted the

1990s study that identified the art in distress. Since then, the organization has recruited volunteers to "adopt" pieces of public art in their communities. The volunteers identify the art in need of restoration and seek out records of its origin, which will obviously help the conservator who is hired to restore it. Many of the volunteers even track down the artists and interview them about the origins of the piece and its components. Save Outdoor Sculpture! volunteers have also established public campaigns to raise money for the restorations. Many nonprofit organizations, including Save Outdoor Sculpture! itself, have been generous in providing grants to the local volunteer groups, helping them get the restoration projects off the ground.

A typical Save Outdoor Sculpture! project was undertaken in Gloucester, Massachusetts, where the bronze statue known as *Gloucester Fisherman* suffered from obvious deterioration. Gloucester, an island just off the Massachusetts coast, endures some very harsh winters, thanks to the strong winds that blow in from the Atlantic Ocean. But Gloucester is also a popular summer resort for thousands of visitors from across the country, giving *Gloucester Fisherman* a special status as the island's most recognizable landmark. Says Pat Weslowski, director of the nonprofit National Memorial Trust, "Symbolically, that statue is of enormous significance for every community that has an outdoor sculpture at risk. Because that statue is so well known, so photographed by thousands of tourists, it could become a major focal point not just in raising public awareness but in seeking long-term solutions to restoring and maintaining outdoor sculptures in all communities."[47]

Sculpted by artist Leonard Craske, *Gloucester Fisherman* has stood on a public square on the island since 1923. It depicts a hardy sailor, dressed in

The sculpture *Gloucester Fisherman* has stood on the island of Gloucester, Massachusetts, since 1923. The community raised funds for the artwork's restoration and upkeep.

SAVING OLD CEMETERIES

*M*ost people do not think of headstones and grave markers (the flat slabs that sit atop graves) as art, but they often do include artistic etchings and even statuary. Many existing headstones and grave markers are hundreds of years old. Many of them have historic value. Like other sculpture displayed outdoors, the stones are often in need of restoration.

That job usually falls to groups of volunteers who "adopt" a local cemetery. The volunteers take charge of the landscaping, keeping the stones from being swallowed up by the overgrowth of plants. That helps preserve the stones, because if they are hidden by shrubs they can be damaged by vehicles, lawn mowers, and other machinery. Says Mary Donahue of the Connecticut Historical Commission, "Stone carving has the same audience as art and architecture, the same conservation concerns for brownstone, marble and brass."

Connecticut is home to nearly five hundred graveyards, many dating back to colonial times. The state has several active volunteer groups that keep the old stones in repair. The stones are often so covered in brush and dirt that radar is employed to find the old graves.

In many areas, local volunteers work on restoring and maintaining old cemeteries like this graveyard in the woods.

Quoted in Eleanor Charles, "Saving Abandoned Cemeteries and Grave Markers," *New York Times*, April 30, 2000.

oilskins, clutching the wheel of a fishing boat. Save Outdoor Sculpture! partnered with a local group, Gloucester United, to raise $5,000 to repair the corroded statue. Gloucester United also pledged to raise $1,500 a year to provide a regular maintenance program for the statue, mostly devoted to the upkeep of a wax coating that protects the statue from the elements.

Indeed, enthusiasm for the restoration project was so high that a separate organization, the Gloucester Fishermen's Wives Association, commissioned a second public sculpture on the island, a statue of the noble wife of the fisherman. The new statue, which was erected near the figure of the fisherman, depicts a woman holding a baby in her arms while a young boy tugs at her skirt. The statue is intended to show the resilient courage of the fisherman's wife, who looks after the home during his times of absence. In this case, the successful conservation of one statue created an enthusiasm in the community that led to the creation of a second work of art.

A Dynamic Field

Public art is part of the fabric of America. The thousands of statues that honor the veterans of the Civil War, the founders of cities, the fishermen of Gloucester and their wives, and the establishment of a Western democracy have unique historical and cultural value. As more communities come to that realization, the art conservator will certainly be called on to provide a valuable public service. There is likely to be a lot of work for conservators in the coming years, but since art is a dynamic field, constantly in the process of changing, art conservators know that the skills and techniques they will need to conserve art in the future are likely to change as well.

Epilogue

The Future of Art Conservation

Art conservation has a past but does it have a future? As technology develops new methods to preserve and protect art, and as artists' materials become more resilient and resistant to the elements, there may come a day when a painting will still look fresh and new even after hanging on a museum wall for hundreds of years. Says Charles S. Tumosa, senior research chemist for the Smithsonian Institution's Center for Materials Research and Education, "What we're trying to do is put our conservator friends out of business."[48]

That day is still very much in the future. In the meantime, the craft and profession of art conservation has changed in the past century and continues to change today. Conservators must be ready to employ new conservation techniques in their work. That is why an educational background in science is regarded as vital for the conservator. In the United States, there are three universities that provide graduate degrees in art conservation—New York University, Buffalo State College, and the University of Delaware—and all three require students to study chemistry.

Other skills are important as well. Since restoration is still part of the job, skills in the fine arts are required. So is a background in art history. Foreign language skills are desirable because conservators often have to travel or confer with experts from other countries. Even all those skills may not be enough. According to Debra Hess Norris, the chair of the art conservation department at the University of Delaware, art conservation is "interdisciplinary from the get-go,"[49] meaning that conservators often work with experts from other fields. Major American museums are already calling on scientists from several disciplines to participate in conservation projects. In California, the Getty Conservation Institute, which is part of the J. Paul Getty Museum, regularly employs archaeologists, geologists, and biologists on conservation projects.

More and more, art conservation will involve computer science and engineering. In photography, for example, digital imaging now dominates the art. Five years ago, that was not the case. Photographic conservators have decades of experience in preserving and restoring negatives and prints that were produced in darkrooms, but they are just learning about the

The Getty Conservation Institute, part of the J. Paul Getty Museum (pictured), works closely with scientists on its art conservation projects.

preservation of digital images, which are typically stored on CD-ROMs and similar media. Not only is a CD-ROM apt to fail, Norris says, but it is possible that further developments in technology will make the CD-ROM obsolete. In the future, will there be hardware available that can access the CD-ROMs and unlock the photographic images they hold? The conservator's job will undoubtedly include finding ways to access old technology.

Says Norris, "We may have to preserve videos and CD-ROMs. That normally isn't the job of the art conservator but the conservator may have to work hand in hand with the engineer. That collaboration has to be broadened. There needs to be more research on what has to be done to preserve these materials. The public thinks a CD-ROM is permanent, but in twenty years you may not be able to read the information on that CD-ROM."[50]

Preserving Culture

Norris and other experts believe that the profession of the art conservator will expand to include ethnographic materials, biological specimens, and other museum exhibits. As the techniques become more refined and based on science, conservators will find that the same measures they employ to repair a sculpture will also work on a tribal mask found in a jungle or a ceramic bowl unearthed during the excavation of an ancient civilization. In fact, the merging of art conservation with the conservation of other antiquities is already happening. At the Smithsonian, the same conservators who work on paintings and sculptures also preserve and restore ancient artifacts.

Sometimes, those artifacts are sealed in jars of formaldehyde. It is estimated that some 2 billion biological specimens are sitting on the shelves of museums and research institutes, some for hundreds of years. A century ago, a biologist who discovered a rare specimen of plant or animal life preserved it with the best-known technology. Now, there is a concern that those preservation techniques have robbed the specimens of information that may be useful to scientists today, such as the

composition of their DNA. Conservators are now asked to find new ways to protect the old specimens so that whatever scientific data they may still hold is preserved for future use.

Some artifacts in need of conservation are far from ancient. At the Smithsonian's National Air and Space Museum, a team of art conservators was called in to restore and preserve several deteriorating aircraft that were on display, including a World War II guided missile. Says Smithsonian Institution secretary Lawrence M. Small,

> The missile's transparent nose cone had been painted over, obscuring the camera that had been installed to help guide it. A chemist worked with a paintings conservator to develop the best solution for removing the nose cone's paint without damaging the plastic underneath. In so doing, [Smithsonian] scientists have allowed researchers and now visitors to see the missile in its entirety, including the camera that marks it as perhaps the earliest example of television's use inside a missile.[51]

The Smithsonian's Air and Space Museum houses the recently restored *Enola Gay*, the World War II aircraft that dropped the atomic bomb on Hiroshima, Japan.

Clearly, the conservation of art is expanding into a widening field that includes conservation of other museum exhibits as well as specimens used in scientific research. The same knowledge and skill employed by the paintings conservator to lift a layer of overpaint from a fresco by Michelangelo was used to peel off the layer of paint slapped onto a missile's nose cone. In both cases, the layers of paint hid significant historical details that were exposed to public inspection thanks to the work of the art conservator. Says Norris, "There is constantly the need for conservation of paintings and decorative art, but there is an increased need for the conservator to focus on natural resources, such as dinosaur bones and plant materials. Conservation is no longer just art conservation—it has become the preservation of culture and natural history."[52]

Notes

Introduction: Why Preserve Art?

1. Quoted in "The Articella," *Medieval Manuscripts in the National Library of Science*. www.nlm.nih.gov/hmd/med ieval/articella.html.
2. Robert G. Bednarik, "The First Stirrings of Creation," *UNESCO Courier*, April 1998. http://cogweb.ucla.edu/ep /art/bednarik_98.html.
3. Daniel Grant, "To Conserve or Not to Conserve," *American Artist*, November 1, 2004, p. 71.
4. James Beck, *Art Restoration*. New York: W.W. Norton, 1993, p. 176.

Chapter 1: The Art and the Science of Conservation

5. Konstanze Bachmann, ed., *Conservation Concerns: A Guide for Collectors and Curators*. Washington, DC: Smithsonian Institution Press, 1992, p. 2.
6. Daniel V. Thompson, *The Materials and Techniques of Medieval Painting*. New York: Dover, 1956, pp. 48–49.
7. Quoted in Harold Holzer, "Saving the 'Imax of Its Day,'" *American Heritage*, August 1, 2005, p. 38.
8. Quoted in Maev Kennedy, "Virgin Canvas Traces Hidden Leonardo Sketch Revealed," *Guardian*, July 1, 2005.
9. Quoted in Ken Gousseau, "Mural Gets $50,000 Facial," *Regina Leader Post*, September 26, 2005.
10. Andrew Oddy, ed., *The Art of the Conservator*. Washington, DC: Smithsonian Institution Press, 1992, p. 19.

Chapter 2: When Good Art Goes Bad

11. Quoted in Fabrizio Mancinelli, "Michelangelo's Frescoes in the Sistine Chapel," in *The Art of the Conservator*, ed. Andrew Oddy. Washington, DC: Smithsonian Institution Press, 1992, p. 93.
12. Quoted in David Jeffrey, "A Renaissance for Michelangelo," *National Geographic*, December 1989, p. 697.
13. David Bomford, *Conservation of Paintings*. London: National Gallery Publications, 1997, p. 33.
14. Bomford, *Conservation of Paintings*, p. 41.
15. Oddy, *Art of the Conservator*, p. 24.
16. Oddy, *Art of the Conservator*, pp. 25–26.
17. Bachmann, *Conservation Concerns*, p. 2.
18. Quoted in Michelle Falkenstein, "The Case of the Escaped Spirit," *Art News*, March 2004, p. 114.
19. Quoted in Falkenstein, "Case of the Escaped Spirit," p. 114.
20. Quoted in Falkenstein, "Case of the Escaped Spirit," p. 114.
21. Quoted in Falkenstein, "Case of the Escaped Spirit," p. 114.

22. Bachmann, *Conservation Concerns*, p. 3.

Chapter 3: How Much Restoration Is Too Much?

23. Rachel Kousser, "Creating the Past: The *Venus de Milo*," *American Journal of Archaeology*, April 2005, p. 235.
24. Knut Nicolaus, *The Restoration of Paintings*. Cologne, Germany: Könemann Verlagsgesellschaft, 1998, p. 257.
25. Nicolaus, *Restoration of Paintings*, p. 260.
26. Bomford, *Conservation of Paintings*, pp. 45–46.
27. Bomford, *Conservation of Paintings*, p. 46.
28. Bomford, *Conservation of Paintings*, p. 71.
29. Beck, *Art Restoration*, p. 40.
30. Beck, *Art Restoration*, p. 65.
31. Quoted in Melinda Henneberger, "Restoration of a Leonardo Is Ruled Out," *New York Times*, February 5, 2002.
32. Quoted in Celestine Bohlen, "Art Scholars Protest a Plan to Restore a Leonardo," *New York Times*, May 23, 2001.
33. Quoted in Henneberger, "Restoration of a Leonardo Is Ruled Out."
34. Quoted in Henneberger, "Restoration of a Leonardo Is Ruled Out."

Chapter 4: Art in Times of Crisis

35. Quoted in Pat R. Gilbert, "The Price of Lost Art; Port Authority Nears Settlement for Pieces Destroyed on 9/11," *Bergen County Record*, April 28, 2003.
36. Donny George Youkahanna, foreword to Milbry Polk and Angela M.H. Schuster, eds., *The Looting of the Iraq Museum, Baghdad: The Last Legacy of Ancient Mesopotamia*. New York:

Harry N. Abrams, 2005, p. 2.
37. Quoted in Barry James, "Thousands of Treasures Said to Be Missing; UNESCO Lengthens List of Looted Art in Iraq," *International Herald Tribune*. www.iht.com/bin/print_ipub. php?file+/articles/2003/05/24/pillage _ed3_2.php.
38. Quoted in Florence Williams, "In Mississippi, History Is Now a Salvage Job," *New York Times*, September 8, 2005.
39. Quoted in Jennifer Odell, "Leonard Loses Thousands of Prints, Saves Negatives in New Orleans," *Down Beat*, p. 26.
40. Quoted in Matt Apuzzo, "Sorting Through Rubble of Art," *Albany Times Union*, October 8, 2005.
41. Chris Stavroudis, "Health and Safety," *Western Association for Art Conservation Newsletter*, September 2005, p. 12.

Chapter 5: Saving Public Art

42. Quoted in Constance Neyer, "Statewide, Ways Sought to Get Sculptures in Shape," *Hartford Courant*, July 7, 1996.
43. Quoted in Gary D. Ford, "An SOS for Outdoor Sculpture," *Southern Living*, October 1997, p. 84.
44. Quoted in Richard Seth Hayden and Thierry W. Despont, *Restoring the Statue of Liberty*. New York: McGraw-Hill, 1986, p. 38.
45. Quoted in Daniel Grant, "Saving Public Sculpture," *American Artist*, August 2000, p. 21.
46. Quoted in Grant, "Saving Public Sculpture," p. 22.
47. Quoted in Andrew Blake, "Weather Taking Toll on Outdoor Sculptures," *Boston Globe*, June 12, 1994.

Epilogue: The Future of Art Conservation

48. Quoted in Jessica Gorman, "Making Stuff Last," *Science News,* December 9, 2000, p. 378.

49. Debra Hess Norris, interview with Hal Marcovitz, January 28, 2006.

50. Norris, interview.

51. Lawrence M. Small, "Reversing the Clock," *Smithsonian,* June 2005, p. 14.

52. Norris, interview.

For Further Reading

Books

James Beck, *Three Worlds of Michelangelo.* New York: W.W. Norton, 1999. The art history professor who led the campaign to halt restoration of the ceiling of the Sistine Chapel turns his attention to the artist who created the magnificent work. The book is a well-researched biography of the Italian artist and includes Beck's interpretation of the clash of wills between Michelangelo and Pope Julius II, who commissioned him to paint the ceiling of the Sistine Chapel.

Kenneth Clark, *Leonardo da Vinci.* New York: Penguin, 1993. Biography of the artist who painted the *Mona Lisa, The Adoration of the Magi,* and many other familiar works of art.

Gregory Curtis, *Disarmed: The Story of the Venus de Milo.* New York: Vintage, 2004. Examines the debate over the origin of the *Venus,* the ownership dispute between France and Germany, and other controversies that surround the world's most famous statue.

Richard Seth Hayden and Thierry W. Despont, *Restoring the Statue of Liberty.* New York: McGraw-Hill, 1986. Written by the architects who headed the restoration of the Statue of Liberty, the book provides a full history of the huge monument as well as a detailed description of the work involved in restoring it. The book includes many photographs and drawings outlining the scope of the work.

Milbry Polk and Angela M.H. Schuster, eds., *The Looting of the Iraq Museum, Baghdad: The Lost Legacy of Ancient Mesopotamia.* New York: Harry N. Abrams, 2005. The book chronicles the ancient art and artifacts stolen or vandalized in the wake of the American-led invasion of Iraq in 2003, providing thorough backgrounds on many artifacts and the roles they played in the history of the Middle East.

Periodicals

Daniel Grant, "Saving Public Sculpture," *American Artist,* August 2000. The article summarizes efforts to preserve outdoor sculpture in America.

Melinda Henneberger, "The Leonardo Cover-Up," *New York Times Sunday Magazine,* April 21, 2002. The feature story chronicles the discovery of sketched images beneath the painted surface of Leonardo da Vinci's *The Adoration of the Magi.*

Harold Holzer, "Saving the 'Imax of Its

Day,'" *American Heritage*, August 1, 2005. Feature article about Paul Philippoteaux's cyclorama depicting the Battle of Gettysburg and the efforts to restore the painting.

David Jeffrey, "A Renaissance for Michelangelo," *National Geographic*, December 1989. The magazine's assistant editor, who visited the conservators at work on the restoration of the ceiling of the Sistine Chapel, gives a short history of Michelangelo's work on the ceiling, tells how the ceiling lost its luster over the years, and explains the techniques that the conservators used to unveil the artist's incandescent colors.

Web Sites

American Institute for Conservation of Historic and Artistic Works (http://aic.stanford.edu/). The organization serves as the national trade association for conservation professionals. Visitors to the institute's Web site can find many articles and resources on art conservation. By accessing the "Caring for Your Treasures" link, students can learn about conservation of paintings, sculpture, architecture, photographs, textiles, and other works of art.

ArtWatch International (www.artwatch international.org) The organization established by Columbia University art history professor James Beck questions conservation projects, challenging museum officials to prove that paintings and other works of art are truly in need of restoration. Visitors to the group's Web site can read about current conservation projects as well as the ArtWatch position on whether the projects are justified.

Cleveland Museum of Art (www.clevelandart.org/exhibcef/picassoas/html/uptc.html). This Web site details the museum's Understanding Picasso Through Conservation project to study the work of artist Pablo Picasso through a scientific analysis that includes examinations with X-rays, infrared reflectography, and a scanning electron microscope.

Conservation Centre at the Liverpool Museum (www.liverpoolmuseums.org.uk/conservation). The conservation arm of the museum in Liverpool, England, maintains an extensive Web site that details many of the museum's restoration projects. By following the link to "Conservation Technologies," students can learn about the use of lasers, 3-D imaging, and other high-tech methods of restoring paintings, sculptures, tapestries, and other works of art.

National Park Service (www.nps.gov/gett/gettprojects/cyclopres03.htm). The National Park Service has established this Web page to explain the project to renovate the Gettysburg cyclorama, the huge painting by Paul Philippoteaux that is being restored and scheduled for rehanging in a new facility at Gettysburg National Military Park in 2007.

Save Outdoor Sculpture! (www.heritage preservation.org/programs/sos/sos main.htm). The organization sponsors restorations of public art in the United States. Visitors can read news updates on projects and download resources that would help them launch campaigns to preserve sculpture in their communities.

Smithsonian Institution Center for Materials Research and Education (SCMRE) (www.si.edu/scmre). SCMRE is the conservation arm of the Washington-based Smithsonian Institution. By accessing the "Learning from Things" link, students can learn about the conservation process as well as the techniques and equipment employed by conservators.

Western Association for Art Conservation (http://palimpsest.stanford.edu/waac). Visitors to the site can download copies of the association's newsletter, which examines many issues in art conservation, including reviews of noted conservation projects, health and safety concerns, and updates on techniques employed by conservators.

Index

Picture Credits

Cover: © Vittoriano Rastelli/ CORBIS

Andreas Gebert/dpa/Landov, 48
AP/Wide World Photos, 13, 16 (main), 18, 20, 21, 33, 37, 73
Art Resource, NY, 62
© Barry Lewis/CORBIS, 83
© Bettmann/CORBIS, 52, 75
© Bob Krist/CORBIS, 31
© Carlo Ferraro/epa/CORBIS, 51
Erich Lessing/Art Resource, NY, 58
© George Steinmetz/CORBIS, 38
Getty Images, 9, 69
HIP/Art Resource, NY 54
© James Marshall/CORBIS, 85
© Kazuyoshi Nomachi/CORBIS, 10
© Larry Dale Gordon/zefa/CORBIS, 44
© Matt Rainey/Star Ledger/CORBIS, 67

© Patrick Robert/CORBIS, 63, 64
© Pete Leonard/zefa/CORBIS, 86
© Philip Gould/CORBIS, 70
© Reuters/CORBIS, 91
Reuters/Landov, 60
© Richard Cummins/CORBIS, 89
© Robert Maass/CORBIS, 80
© Roger Wood/CORBIS, 16 (inset)
© Sandro Vannini/CORBIS, 23
Scala/Art Resource, NY, 15, 26, 50
© SETBOUN/CORBIS, 41
© Stephanie Diani/CORBIS, 24
© Steve Raymer/CORBIS, 28
Tamia Dowlatabadi, 27, 43, 56
The New York Public Library/Art Resource, NY, 77
© Vittoriano Rastelli/CORBIS, 34, 55
© Wally McNamee/CORBIS, 39

About the Author

Hal Marcovitz is a journalist and the author of more than seventy books for young readers. He lives in Chalfont, Pennsylvania, with his wife Gail and daughters Ashley and Michelle.